GHOST
WORLDS

A GUIDE TO POLTERGEISTS, PORTALS, ECTO–MIST & SPIRIT BEHAVIOR

GHOST
WORLDS

MELBA GOODWYN

Llewellyn Publications
Woodbury, Minnesota

First Edition
First Printing, 2007

Book design by Steffani Sawyer
Cover design by Kevin R. Brown
Cover tree image by Carsten Leuzinger/imagebroker/Alamy Limited
Editing by Jane Hilkin
Llewellyn is a registered trademark of Llewellyn Worldwide, Ltd.

Library of Congress Cataloging-in-Publication Data for *Ghost Worlds: A
Guide to Poltergeists, Portals, Ecto-Mist & Spirit Behavior* is on file at the
Library of Congress.
        ISBN: 978-0-7387-1195-9

Llewellyn Publications
A Division of Llewellyn Worldwide, Ltd.
2143 Wooddale Drive, Dept. 978-0-7387-1195-9
Woodbury, Minnesota 55125-2989, U.S.A.
www.llewellyn.com

Printed in the United States of America

ACKNOWLEDGMENTS

Exploring the realm of paranormal investigations has been an exciting experience. Being clairvoyant, I have always readily accepted the fact that we can, and do, communicate with discarnate souls. I have spent my entire life in communication, in one form or another, with entities in other realms of existence. However, although this is very easy for me, I never entertained the idea of, nor felt the need for, proof of their existence. They just were!

Robert Kolodzik and Kathy James… Thank you, Robert and Kathy. Without you there may not have been a *first* ghost hunt. Your expertise and humor as well as your patient instruction made it possible for me to expand my psychic awareness and provided me with even further proof, beyond a shadow of a doubt, that *there is no death, and we do not die.*

Sharon Howe… Thank you for your constant support, your laughter, and, most of all, your never-ending "ghost-hunting" enthusiasm.

Ricky Joe Goodwin and Christy Bates… Thank you for your love and support and your enthusiastic motivation on our ghost hunts. Bless you both.

Kay Ainsworth…My ghost-busting buddy and my own personal cheerleader. No matter what new, weird, odd, or unusual adventure I embark upon, I always have your support! A special thank you! Also, Katie, I would like to express my heartfelt appreciation for sharing your time, energy, and expertise throughout the process of writing this book.

Franklin Long…Thank you, Franklin, for allowing me to experience my spirituality in all its varied forms. Your support means everything to me.

Tamatha Williams…I can never thank you enough for your empowering love and affection as well as your energetic assessment of our psychic gifts and talents and your willingness to explore life with me.

Douglas and Gloria Perry…You are great! Thanks for all your love and support as we ventured through our portal of understanding. Douglas, your ghost-questing spirit is amazing!

Jane Cheatham…Thank you for your encouragement and your sincere belief in my writing talent!

And last, but by no means least, many thanks to *Mitchel Whitington*, writer and friend who read the manuscript for this book and gave me invaluable assistance and guidance. To say I appreciate you is simply not enough!

Happy Ghosting!

Melba Goodwyn

ABOUT THE AUTHOR

Melba Goodwyn is an experienced parapsychologist and shares her psychic impressions with local police departments as well as individuals interested in ghost hunting. Blending clairvoyant wisdom with traditional psychology, she has provided spiritual counseling for over twenty-five years. She uses her knowledge of astrology, numerology and divination to assist others and enhance their spirituality.

CONTENTS

INTRODUCTION

My first recollection of ghosts came at the age of five while I was visiting my paternal grandmother in the early 1950s. She lived deep in the woods of East Texas and was never at a loss for words when it came to telling ghost stories. She was also clairvoyant, and I'm sure this enabled her to see and hear more than most.

Late one afternoon as we were sitting on her front porch, I saw a huge puff of smoky mist encircling her favorite gardenia bush. Already seduced by the fragrant smell of the flowers and a lazy afternoon, I wondered if I was really seeing what appeared to be floating all around the bush. When I told her what I was seeing, she just smiled at me and said, "Oh, that's just a haint, it don't mean you no harm." I was fascinated by the way it appeared very dense and then in the next instant willowy and wispy. It could change direction at will and just as easily change form, and then suddenly it just disappeared into the fast approaching darkness of a sleepy Texas sky.

My second experience came at the age of ten, while I was squirrel hunting with my dad. We left home very early in the morning, and although I had begged for weeks for Dad to take me with him, I wasn't prepared for the cold, damp, eerie woods we encountered. I had promised to be quiet, which was an overwhelming task that took every ounce of self-restraint I had. Then we saw them! Suddenly, there appeared before us three huge, thick, white forms floating in between and around the trees in the thicket. I have to tell you I let out a scream that shook the leaves on the trees. These white entities stretched out until they were very long and then drew themselves back up into huge, elongated oval shapes. I was stunned beyond words, which was amazing in and of itself. Dad, however, remained calm, and I thought to myself that he was the bravest man on the face of the earth. He quietly explained to me that they were the ghosts of men who had died and that they meant us no harm. We stood there watching them watching us, for what seemed like an eternity. Then, just as quickly as they appeared, they evaporated into the damp morning air! I'm afraid my father didn't accomplish any serious hunting, as I was constantly looking over my shoulder and walking into trees. I realize now that Dad was also clairvoyant, although he kept this well hidden from everyone most of his life. *"They mean us no harm!"* This was the message I received from both my grandmother and my father. So with this in mind, let's explore the realm of ghosts.

I believe that everyone, at some point in their lives, has had an encounter of some kind with a ghost. It may have come as a visual sighting, such as mine, or it may have been heard, felt, or only sensed as goose bumps. No matter how you may have experienced a ghostly presence, rest assured ghosts do exist. They do try to communicate with us, they do appear as various forms and shapes, and last, but not least, they mean us no harm.

My accounts of ghosts, discarnate souls existing as spiritual energy, are being written from what I believe to be a different perspective than most. It is written from my perspective as a clairvoyant, clairaudient psychic. As I sprinkle my writing with accounts of my personal experiences, you may recognize phenomena you have encountered at times. I would like to offer my psychic perspective, which stems from my own clairvoyant awareness of vibrations, frequencies, and spiritual energies, as well as other dimensions beyond our own.

Many ghost hunters are strictly after the thrill of the chase. Anxious to be scared out of their wits, they relish having a ghost story to tell others. Admittedly this is fun and exciting; however, it loses its luster in the light of spiritual understanding. It is this spiritual understanding that I seek. I feel that we should reach beyond the mere thrill of the hunt and strive to understand the connection between our two dimensions.

Still others come from a very strict research perspective and seek to understand the phenomena they encounter, using scientific criteria in their efforts to discern and explain what a ghost is. However, when scientific research methods are applied, any concept of the spiritual nature of the very thing being investigated can be lost. We all encounter mysterious, unusual events and circumstances in our lives. We all sense things, we all hear things, and we all see things. We always know on a deeper level that what we have encountered has meaning and purpose in our lives. There are no coincidences, and, if we feel a ghostly presence, it's because we are meant to.

Exploring other realms, ghosts, and paranormal activity can be fun, exciting, and enlightening, if you are spiritually aware of what is going on. Combining fun, excitement, research, and investigation with spiritual understanding will lead the ghost hunter to the ultimate paranormal experience. Acceptance of ghosts as spiritual energy presenting itself as vibrations and frequencies that can be seen, felt, and heard can alter our understanding of paranormal events dramatically.

It is this ultimate experience that I seek on a daily basis and wish for each and every one of my readers.

Happy Ghosting!
Melba Goodwyn

ONE

DO YOU BELIEVE IN GHOSTS?

Oh, Heaven, it is mysterious,
it is awful to consider that we not only carry
a future ghost within us; but are, in very deed, Ghosts!

THOMAS CARLYLE (1795–1881)

Ghosts and things that go bump in the night! The very thought of these things can send shivers up and down your spine!

Simply put, a "belief" in ghosts is almost inherent within us. From childhood to adulthood, most of us carry a memory of "ghosts" with us. These ghosts may have appeared in books or movies, as stories told by our grandparents, or as actual visitations. It doesn't matter how we were introduced to ghosts, the fact remains that it was probably a memorable event. If it was an actual sighting, it undoubtedly impressed itself on your psyche, never to be forgotten. Anyone who has ever seen a ghost swears they'll never forget the experience.

Remembered are ghosts that we will never forget; indeed, if you have seen one, you can't forget it! Childhood ghost stories are stored in most of our memories, and any account of ghosts seen by our friends or family members stays with us all our lives. Ghosts we have personally seen, heard, felt, or sensed seem to follow us as shadows that never fade from our memories. Even though these visitors from another dimension may cause us to question our sanity, they are and will always remain our unseen companions as we journey through life.

Remember the *Leave It to Beaver* sitcom from the '50s? Ward Cleaver was trying to ease Beaver's fear of ghosts by telling him that there was no such thing as a ghost. Beaver's response was "Well, why do they have a name then?" I agree totally with his perception. Why indeed! Because they do exist!

I do believe in ghosts, and in this book I will present my best evidence and leave it up to my readers to form their own opinions. I realize that some people will deny the validity of my concepts no matter how strong the evidence. That's fine. I will simply state my evidence as clearly as possible and allow it to speak for itself.

In searching for answers about what ghosts are, we can eliminate a long list of what they are not. Scientists can't define them and neither can religion (which cannot even fully explain the journey of the soul). Why not? Because they would have to admit that ghosts are real. If we can't admit that they exist, how can we ever begin to accept them as part of our reality? So where does that leave us? We must rely on our own innate intuition and spirituality. Spirituality, by my definition, entails trusting our intuition, seeing what we believe, and accepting the truth as it surfaces from deep within our souls.

Since the age of five, I have been aware of ghosts and spirits. As I grew older I became aware of my guides. I grew to trust them and the messages they imparted to me. I often turn to them when I have questions regarding ghosts and their existence. They are always willing to share their opinions and information and have answered many questions regarding energy, vibrations, and discarnate entities. They have very gently led me to a higher understanding of dimensional frequencies and vibrational energies, as well as ghosts and their various forms of manifestation. Information received from my guides through my clairvoyant perception, coupled with technical ghost-hunting equipment, has cemented my belief about ghosts and spirits residing in other dimensions, yet ever present in our own.

Although I am clairvoyant, I have the same experiences as everyone else and share the same emotions. I have an overwhelming need to know the truth even when that truth leads me far from the safe boundaries of blissful ignorance.

A recent Gallup poll has revealed that 32 percent of all adult Americans believe in ghosts and 37 percent say that they believe houses can be haunted. One half of the nation believes in some kind of paranormal phenomenon. So if you're reading this and wondering if you are alone in your belief, you are not. Ghosts do exist!

People often ask me if I see ghosts. The answer is yes. A lot of my interaction with spirits and ghosts comes about because they appear with a client during a session. They want their loved ones to know that they are happy and capable of communicating with them. On one occasion when a client arrived for a reading, she appeared with two guests. This is often the case, so I didn't anticipate anything unusual. As they gathered in the sitting room, I left to retrieve another chair so all of them could sit comfortably. My client and her friend looked at me with very confused expressions on their faces. My client asked me why I had brought another chair into the room, why I needed three chairs when there were only two of them. Obviously I was seeing a third party who had arrived with them but from another dimension. To me she appeared as real and solid as they were. The reading turned out to be very emotional as well as self-empowering for my client.

If you grasp the concept that ghosts were once human, it's easy to understand that even in death they never leave us. Human consciousness indeed survives death and resides in an unseen dimension interwoven with ours, a dimension that is just a whisper away from our loved ones.

Ghosts have been written about for centuries and more recently portrayed in Hollywood movies (albeit in a scary sense). However, many people have had extraordinary, undeniable encounters with a ghostly presence. Hundreds of people encounter ghosts every day (or night) in their own homes, in parks and cemeteries, at their workplaces, schools, in medical buildings, and at historical sites around the country. And why not? They have as much right to be there as we do.

Ghostly visitations have been a part of human life throughout all of recorded history and without a doubt long before that. Especially remembered, recorded, and saved for posterity are visions and encounters that inspire and illuminate one's spirituality.

In general, those of us who believe in ghosts also believe that we are created as two very distinct energy systems coming together to form a whole unit: one is physical (condensed energy) and the other spiritual (ethereal energy). Our ability to manifest as a ghost is based on our spiritual body's vibrational frequencies, which will be explained in upcoming chapters.

How one perceives a ghost is somewhat dependent upon cultural background. However, ghosts are seen and reported with such consistency in shape and form that there can be little doubt of their existence. I believe that we have no alternative but to accept them as part of our ever-changing perception of reality.

The subject of ghosts is one of the most interesting as well as controversial forms of paranormal activity. They are subjected to a great deal of religious debunking and open skepticism. Ghosts are not figments of our imagination, though, nor are they demons floating in ecto-mist. They simply are!

Tremendous growth in interest about ghosts alerts me to the fact that it is time for the unseen to be seen and time for the mysterious unknown to become known and accepted.

Do you believe in ghosts? Perhaps a more appropriate question would be: "Are you prepared to admit that you believe in ghosts?"

TWO

HAUNTINGS PAST AND PRESENT

All houses in which men have lived and died
Are haunted houses.
Through the open doors
The harmless phantoms on their errands glide
With feet that make no sound upon the floor.

HENRY WADSWORTH LONGFELLOW (1807–1882)

What many people believe to be a haunting may not necessarily be due to a ghostly presence at all, and not everyone who visits a place reported to be haunted will have
an experience with a ghost. The word *haunt* indicates a
ghostly visitation that occurs constantly over a period of
time. Typically, a haunted location is the former home of
a deceased person or the place where they died. However,
that is not always the case, as ghosts apparently haunt the
places that they frequented or favored in life. They may be
there because of their connection to that site or to the people who are living there.

When ghost hunters receive a call from homeowners or clients, they will interview them and then begin an
investigation to determine the real cause of the haunting.
What the homeowner may be experiencing or sensing is a
residual energy imprint of the previous owner.

Houses retain tremendous amounts of energy. Have
you ever noticed how quickly a house will deteriorate after
a family moves away or the previous owner dies? There is
simply not enough energy to sustain it. However, if you see
a house that has stood the test of time, you can rest assured
that there is still a very powerful energy actively maintaining that dwelling.

Many old structures have survived for decades or even
centuries. They include but are not limited to churches,
schoolhouses, huge old homes, hospitals, and courthouses.
They are all storehouses for electromagnetic energy. These
various structures were the centers of activity, the hustle
and bustle of life. This is especially true of very old houses.

Every conceivable form of community or family event could have been held in people's homes. From social gatherings such as teas and quilting bees to political meetings and funerals, these events and the emotions that defined them have left their energy imprints on the very soul of the structure. Imprints may be picked up for years, and possibly forever, by those who seek them. Consider the various energy imprints that would have been made over a few generations in a family home. There would surely have been good times and bad. There would have most likely been joyous family occasions such as weddings and births. But there also would have been sad energies released in the home during times of family grief. For instance, in times past, it was the custom to place a deceased person's body in the drawing room and hold the funeral right there at home. What an imprint a room full of mourning people must have had on those walls!

Other, more horrifying events took place in homes and various structures. Any place where an extremely emotionally charged event happened probably holds that energy today. Rapes, murders, suicides—any event that creates a sense of terror in the human heart leaves that highly charged energy where it was emitted. And thus we find…a haunted place.

Sometimes a soul may just be reluctant to leave. It may not want to relinquish its desire to be near the home it loved, the place that holds all its cherished memories of the past. As a ghost, that soul may enjoy familiar surroundings much the same as you and I, thus making their hold on the home even more powerful.

Where do you spend most of your time in your home? Is it in the den, the kitchen, bedroom, workshop, on the porch, or perhaps outside in the garden? Ghosts are there too…watching you! These are also the places where you leave a strong energy imprint while going through your daily routine of everyday life. These imprints can and will be picked up by others in the future.

A ghost hunter or paranormal investigator may be challenged when having to discern whether the homeowner has a ghost, or simply smells, feels, senses, or intuits a previous occupant's energy.

If you stumble upon or receive a call about a well-maintained house or building that is extremely old and still in good repair, my guess is that more than likely one or more ghosts will be in residence. Sometimes it's easy to recognize a haunted place by its condition. It's safe to say that an old deserted house or building that should be falling in on itself but isn't, has a few ghostly energies keeping it up. Their energy alone will help keep their living quarters safe from the ravages of time.

This was the case with an investigation our team did of an elegant old antebellum home. Even though it was built over 180 years ago and has been vacant and mostly neglected for many years, it is in remarkably good shape. The reason why? A very strong and masterful ghostly presence that still lives there.

We arrived before dark so we could familiarize ourselves with the house and the surrounding grounds. We were met by the caretakers, a lovely couple, who had a deep appreciation for the history of the house and the families who had lived there.

Before the actual investigation began, we were given a tour of the grounds surrounding the house. This tour revealed many interesting facts about the house and its previous owners. In the back of the house were two outbuildings. One building contained an old cistern and was kept locked for safety purposes. The other building yielded a wealth of information. What a surprise upon entering it to see four tombstones lying on the dark, musty dirt floor of the building! Two of the stones were broken in half. When I asked the caretakers where they came from, they could offer little information other than the fact that they probably belonged to the original owners.

Although the names were different, I was intrigued by the fact that they were there. I surmised that members of the family were probably buried there, and in an attempt to hide the family plot, they erected a building over the graves. In-depth research after the investigation revealed that four family members were buried on the property and the tombstones had been visible for years. No one is clear when or why they were hidden, but this does seem to be the case.

Daylight was fading fast as we approached the area where the slave quarters once stood. Although now an open field, I sensed a lot of energy and suspected that this area could be a hotbed of activity.

Rushing to savor the last bit of daylight, we approached the house. As we gathered near the back door, the caretakers related to us that the original owner had died in the house and was buried beneath a huge old magnolia tree near the side of the house. Although there was no marker to establish exactly where he was buried, the fact that he was buried there was beyond dispute, as it had been recorded and reported over a century ago.

Later that night, my son Douglas and I ventured outside to photograph that enormous magnolia tree. We captured on film what I believe to be a ghost. It appeared suddenly from underneath the tree and glowed with acknowledgment. Perhaps it was the original owner's way of saying hello.

We entered the house and were given a brief tour of the rooms. I expected a huge old empty house and was not prepared to step back in time over one hundred years. My perception changed dramatically as I was swept into the past. The house was filled to the brim with antique furniture, glassware, pictures, knickknacks, and books, books, and more books. I was stunned! It was as if the family had just walked away and never looked back.

Of course everything was in a state of disarray. Things seemed to be scattered, displaced, and otherwise disarranged. Many things were covered with sheets, dusty with age. The walls were still covered with the original wallpaper although it was coming down in places. However, this only added to the ambiance of the house.

Everyone present during the investigation was in awe of the regal and stately beauty of the house. The men on our team were fascinated with the construction, commenting that it looked as if it had been built only a few years ago. The floors were sturdy, and even the attic was very well maintained.

All the other team members except me were up in the attic praising some unknown carpenter from the past, when the already noticeable paranormal activity accelerated. Noises and eerie sounds could be heard. Doors were slamming somewhere in the house, and footsteps could be heard ascending the stairs. Suddenly, loud whooshing sounds sent them flying downstairs a lot faster than they went up. (Of course, later that night they had to bite the bullet and go back up to the attic to retrieve their equipment!) Before the night was over they had gathered much more evidence than they had anticipated.

Throughout the night, we visited room after room and documented many anomalies. The activity was increasing the longer we stayed. One particular ghost was so strong that I felt him touch my shoulder and I heard his voice.

At one point during the investigation, the team decided to go upstairs to a room where the owner had been "sensed" on several occasions. Sharon, one of the team members, is adept at using dowsing rods, so it was decided that she would attempt to communicate with him. During the question-and-answer session, she asked if anyone else wanted to ask any questions. The caretaker laughed and said, "I have a question." He then asked point-blank, "Where is the money?"

I had chosen to stay downstairs in the parlor to review the pictures on my digital camera. There was a huge old rocker that seemed to welcome me with open arms. Little did I realize that it was really an invitation for a visitation! As I sat there sensing the aura of the house, I felt someone touch my shoulder ever so lightly. I shivered as I realized that I was not alone. Then I heard a male voice say, "Are you looking for my money?" Of course I didn't have a clue as to what he was talking about, and I'm sure my nervous reply of "Oh, no" was a sure indication to him that I was merely an observer in his world. As I was trying to regain my composure, I heard him say, "Then you are welcome." I sat there in stunned silence, almost afraid to move. Although I didn't see him I could sense his strong personality.

I called to the others and told them what had happened. We were all excited because one of our cameras was pointed directly at the rocking chair. We just knew we had caught the ghost on film, but unfortunately, the film didn't reveal the ghost. However, we do know without a doubt that this old house has at least one powerful ghost to ensure its longevity. I also think that it is very significant that the same subject—money—was what was on the ghost's mind. Whether or not there is any money or treasure there, it is obvious that the old master of that estate doesn't want to give up his attachment to his worldly goods.

Although the inside was definitely haunted, the outside was a hotbed of activity. We were able to photograph many energy anomalies, a sure indication of a ghostly presence. We are all eagerly anticipating a return visit this fall when cooler weather will make our investigation easier.

As in this case, ghosts can become very attached to their dwellings. Regardless of whether it's a house or building, I can assure you that they believe their right of ownership excludes everyone else's.

Any ghost hunter will probably be viewed as an intruder, especially with all the unfamiliar equipment and gadgets we use. The ghosts may try to scare us away. If they are successful in making us fearful, they will win on two counts. First, we leave, and secondly, they are able to absorb fear energy, which empowers them.

Often, ghost hunters will receive a call when a homeowner has begun renovations. These remodeling plans can create confusing and frightening scenes if the resident ghost doesn't want or like the changes being made in its home. Annoyed by the changes being made, a ghost may cause many disruptive disturbances and may create some pretty scary scenarios that make the homeowner's life difficult and miserable.

Remember, although they are ghosts now, they have lived here before, perhaps their entire lives, and they do not want to leave. The more apprehensive you become, the more the ghost will benefit from your fears.

After we have ascertained what is going on and what or who is causing the problem, we are then ready to talk to the homeowner or client. They will want to know what they can do, if they do indeed have a ghost. We can help them understand the situation and explain the ghosts' behavior. Of course it is their choice as to how they prefer to handle it. Understanding that a ghost is a person may be hard for some people, especially if they have had a very strict religious indoctrination or if they are highly skeptical and analytical. However, that does not negate the fact that ghosts are people as real as you and me, although invisible to us.

As investigators, we can identify the sources of the paranormal activity and either disavow or validate the home owner's perception of what is going on. Beyond that we are limited as to what we can do.

It is never a good idea to attempt to "evict" a ghost, unless the ghost hunter is experienced and confident that they are capable of this. To do otherwise would seriously damage one's integrity and credibility as a paranormal investigator. The ghosts may have grown so content with their surroundings over the years that they simply will not leave. After all, they could have been there for hundreds of years, either in the structure or on the land (which could have been haunted for centuries).

My suggestion is to sit down and talk to the ghost. Be sincere and explain your feelings. Ask them to either leave or share the space benevolently. More often than not, this will work. The ghost will get the recognition it craves, and you will have the peace of mind of knowing that although you have a ghost in the house, you can coexist. At this point some people would rather move and leave their situation to be explained by the next unsuspecting homeowner.

Ghost hunters will usually receive a distress call when the client or home owner starts to experience one or more of the following on a consistent basis:

Some of the first signs of a ghostly presence are smells and aromas from an undetermined source. Floral fragrances are among the most prominent. However, cigar smoke, liquor smells, and perfumes run a close second.

People may begin to hear sounds and noises that have not been heard before. These may manifest as phantom footsteps, rappings, and knocks and bumps heard throughout the night. Daytime experiences of sound may include music being heard as well as laughter and whispers. It is not at all unusual to hear someone call your name and then turn to see that no one is there. A very disconcerting event is to be awakened by screams in the middle of the night. This is not uncommon.

Finally, homeowners may experience one or more of the following: furniture being moved, lights flickering on and off, doors opening and closing, as well as televisions and other appliances malfunctioning. All of these things can be very unsettling.

However, to see a misty form of a ghost in your home or catch a glimpse of someone's shadow out of your peripheral vision is shocking, to say the least. To witness such an event can cause you to question your sanity! But to see a full-bodied apparition (face to face) could without a doubt cause one considerable distress.

When seeing an apparition or ghost, they may appear as they looked while they were alive. They will probably appear in the style of dress reminiscent of the age or era they lived in. As ghosts, they are also capable of revealing themselves to you in a nonthreatening way, one that is acceptable to you. This all depends on the ghost, its mission or purpose for being there, and the message, if any, it wishes to convey.

Although ghosts are generally associated with old houses, they naturally inhabit many other locations. One of the first places most people expect to be haunted is a cemetery. Why? Because the body is there! But, the body is *not* the soul. Therefore, as a disembodied soul, it is capable of travel, visitations, and otherwise being wherever it wants to be, whenever it chooses to be there.

CEMETERIES

History is full of stories of haunted cemeteries. We've all read about eerie ghosts wandering around in graveyards on a moonlit night and shrouded misty figures floating across tombstones. These illusions are usually enough to make even die-hard ghost hunters a little nervous.

Surprisingly, most cemeteries are not haunted. If they are, it is probably due to one of two reasons. First, it is possible the site was haunted long before the cemetery was ever established there. Our ancestors could have been intuitively drawn to that area because it was representative of accumulated energy. For instance, Native Americans chose their burial grounds in this manner. Perhaps unconsciously they were led to take their people to a place that was closely connected to other realms. The land itself could have also been the site of a portal. Thus they honored their dead by energizing their souls.

The second reason is that cemeteries are places that carry imprints of deep emotions. We go to cemeteries to reaffirm our love for the people we have lost, to seek closure, and to reflect on our own mortality. These emotions alone are enough to entice ghostly manifestations. Remember, ghosts resonate to frequencies that are similar to their own. So they could very easily respond to feelings of great sadness or peace and joy as well.

Cemeteries can seem very eerie at night. Many anomalous photographs have been taken in the dark as well as in the daytime. It is always advisable to notify the groundskeeper and get permission to enter a cemetery after dark, especially if it is gated.

TAVERNS

Take it from an ex-bartender: any place that serves alcohol, provides companionship, and creates an atmosphere of fun and excitement is a prime location for odd, unusual characters. I have certainly seen my share! Dead and alive!

Historically, there are many old barrooms, saloons, taverns, and speakeasies that still harbor ghosts of long ago. From cowboys to gangsters, ghosts linger to savor a taste of the past. Of course, over the years many people have died as a result of barroom fights, shoot-outs, and mob massacres. Unfortunately, these often happened in bars, saloons, and taverns, as well as restaurants that serve liquor.

When investigating a bar or places that used to be speakeasies, saloons, or ballrooms for that matter, it would be very beneficial to research the history of the building or site. Always ask to see the basement, if possible, or any storage rooms or hidden spaces as well. These places are often the oldest parts of a building and have escaped serious renovations over the years. They could be the repository of ageless energies in the form of a ghost or residual energy.

HOTELS AND BOARDINGHOUSES

It appears that almost every historic hotel or old boardinghouse, no matter how old, has a resident ghost. Many hotels exploit their ghosts, taking advantage of the publicity, thereby creating a mysterious ghostly atmosphere for their guests and ghost hunters as well. And who doesn't want to spend the night in a haunted hotel, right?

Our team spent a weekend at a haunted hotel in Jefferson, Texas. The entire top floor was rented to ghost hunters. What an exciting trip! The hotel was established in the 1870s and has a rousing history to complement its ghostly persona. The hotel staff was very accommodating and the people in town were extremely friendly and helpful.

Hotel ghost hunts can be a lot of fun. More often than not the hotel's staff will be happy to accommodate ghost hunters by opening up their "haunted rooms" for inspection. One of my best photographs was taken as we were checking out of the haunted Jefferson Hotel. As I passed a room, I felt an unusual presence. There was no one around other than the maid who was cleaning the room. I asked her if she would mind if I took a few pictures. She was very pleasant and allowed me access to the room. I have a very big, densely textured blue orb covered with ecto-mist that I caught sitting on a chair, apparently watching the maid as she worked. I thanked the maid for her courtesy, and I was more than happy when she shared some of the hotel's secret ghost stories with me.

During our stay in Jefferson, we took an excellent ghost tour. We also visited many antique stores that projected their own sense of history and times long past. The entire town's ambiance takes on a peaceful, mysterious glow after dark. We caught a full apparition on film after dark. While wandering around about 3:00 in the morning, investigator Christy Bates took two enthralling photographs. One was of a tall tower of ecto-mist and the other was the ghost of what appears to be a Confederate soldier wandering the streets of Jefferson, Texas. The hotel had revealed many interesting energy anomalies, orbs, and ecto-mists, but none as impressive as these apparitions.

Boardinghouses and hotels, as well as motels, are places where huge amounts of energy are stored. Many traumatic events have happened in these buildings: murders, suicides, in addition to other untimely deaths. These tragic events will often leave an imprint for years to come, and of course ghosts could choose to remain as well.

Look for haunted hotels; they are great getaways for a weekend of ghost hunting. And don't forget to ask the local people about nearby cemeteries or other haunted locations they may know about.

THEATERS

Most opera houses and theaters have a ghost or two in-house, and some have many. The excitement, pleasure, and entertainment seem to draw them, especially if they resonate to a particular actor or actress. Ghosts love a good time and the theater represents fun and excitement.

If you are fortunate enough to gain entrance to an old theater or opera house, check out the balconies, the basement, and the dressing rooms or where they used to be. A lot of your photographs may reveal that ghosts want to be near the action. The stage is a major enticement to ghosts, as scenes are played out and emotions are portrayed. Perhaps a ghost is acting out a part right alongside the actors but is invisible to the audience.

MUSEUMS

Antiques and treasured items may be associated with ghostly activity. The objects move around when no one is near. Curators and cleaning staff alike have reported strange occurrences, such as eerie sounds and light anomalies, in rooms where objects are displayed. These bizarre events can be related to almost any object, such as jewelry, books, dolls, clocks, furniture, or crystal balls.

If the past owner had a strong attachment or emotional connection to an object, they can return to be near it, to secure its safety, and even in rare instances move it to a new location. Although it is a rare event when things disappear out of locked cases, it is not unheard of.

Taking pictures in museums will probably be prohibited. However the grounds surrounding the exhibits may reveal astonishing energy forms or anomalies. This is especially true if you are visiting an outside museum or collection of exhibits.

ABANDONED PRISONS AND JAILS

Remembering that violence and extremes of emotion create areas of paranormal phenomena, it is no wonder that prisons or old jailhouses are hotbeds of activity. Old jails and abandoned prisons are plentiful and you may be able to gain access to them. These sites and locations may not be to everyone's liking, but they could produce solid evidence of ghosts. With their history of violence, pain, and anger, there should be enough ghostly activity to satisfy any ghost hunter's quest for the unknown.

LARGE COMMUNITY BUILDINGS

Bus stations, train stations, old department store buildings, and courthouses are all reservoirs of paranormal energies. Old buildings such as these retain the electromagnetic energies of all the people who have passed through their doors, year after year, decade after decade, and possibly century after century. If a building was a place of constant activity, it is very possible that ghosts have chosen to reside there. The huge open areas and lobbies are conducive to ghostly manifestations of all kinds and could easily become Grand Central Station for any number of spirits and ghosts.

After years of activity, these old buildings and businesses may have found other uses, and the ghosts may belong to other eras. They may appear wearing clothing from another time period to startle unsuspecting visitors.

You may see the ghosts of people who worked there, such as clerks, elevator attendants, ticket agents, or simply people who went about their daily affairs while entering and exiting the building.

Remember: when on an investigation, try not to overlook areas that could have once been very busy with activity; double-check rooms that could have served as offices, lobbies, reception areas, ticket booths, and concessions. As always, check out the basement and attics even though they may be used for storage now; they could have had many other uses in the past.

ACCIDENT AND CRIME SCENES

These sites and locations are infamous for accounts of paranormal activity and ghosts. Investigations and research at sites such as these may be eerie; you may find that you are overwhelmed with emotion. The emotion you experience at the scene of a murder or horrific accident may leave you feeling weak and confused. If this happens, it is important to remember that you may only be sensing the energies left behind by the people who were involved. There may not be a ghost present.

As a ghost hunter, you may one day receive a call to investigate a crime scene. This request may come from a parent or family member of the victim or from a law enforcement agent, especially if they can be assured of your discretion and professionalism. Respect everyone's feelings; be prepared to counsel their concerns and console them if necessary. You may be expected to discuss death and dying.

If you are not prepared to do this, then please avoid these encounters.

The ghosts of the victims may appear; however, they will probably be in a residual state and may not be aware that they have been transformed. If family members are present, do not be too quick to reveal all that you see, hear, or film and record. Allow some time for you to process what has taken place; this will give the family time to deal with their emotions. You may want to meet later at another location that would be more appropriate for sharing the results of your investigation. Again, this may be traumatic for the family members, so be very professional and discreet when relating to them what you learned at the site.

BATTLEFIELDS

Civil War battlefields tend to be some of the most haunted sites in the United States, with Gettysburg appearing to be the most haunted of all.

Excellent evidence has been documented at battlefields by paranormal researchers and ghost hunters. The tremendous amount of pain, suffering, fear, and death may have left unforgettable imprints in the surrounding areas. Look for old forts, prisons, barns, sheds, in fact any building in close proximity to a battlefield as they may contain the ghosts of soldiers who fought and died there. Any building that could have been used as a makeshift hospital or morgue most likely harbors ghosts. Survey the area for these buildings and try to determine if they would warrant an investigation.

The violent confrontations that took place in battle zones surely produced hundreds of ghosts. These ghost soldiers may continue to fight battles in their own indistinct dimensions. You may hear or see them; you may even smell the stench of the dead and dying. If you are faced with overwhelming emotions, leave the site and come back later. Believe it or not, having to deal with one's emotions during a ghost hunt or investigation is very common and often very necessary.

As these battles were fought out in the open, atmospheric effects may activate a ghostly manifestation or materialization at the site. The cooler months of fall and winter offer an abundance of paranormal activities. These are also very good months for planning field trips and investigations.

HOSPITALS AND ASYLUMS

Hospitals and nursing homes are probably some of the most haunted places you will ever encounter on an investigation. Deaths and emotional traumas occur almost daily. So many emotions are experienced that it's no wonder they are haunted. Fear, confusion, dread, pain, and misery all entangle to create an atmosphere of repressed energy. Ghosts have been reported to walk the halls and visit nurses stations; call buttons come on when there is no one in the rooms; furniture moves on its own accord; beds go up and down; chairs rock. The phenomena is endless and very unnerving to those who work there.

If you investigate an abandoned nursing home, hospital, or asylum, be prepared to experience new emotions. These feelings may be shocking to you, as you will be absorbing the memories of patients and their families. If you are very sensitive or clairvoyant, you may want to consider avoiding these places, as the energies could overload your psyche. You will probably see many ghosts (who will also see you) who want to communicate with you, thereby demanding your attention.

Asylums are tragic places that carry enormous amounts of electromagnetic energy. Many of the people who were confined there were literally trapped by physical or mental problems that did not allow them free expression of their energy. What happened to all that repressed energy? It was projected into the atmosphere of the asylum. If there is any one place where bizarre, unusual energy anomalies are found, this is it. Ghosts continuously walk the halls of abandoned asylums, lost in the darkness of their inner prisons.

CAVES

Can old mine shafts, caves, and tunnels have a ghost? Yes, of course!

However, investigating these areas, unless they are publicly accessible, can be very hazardous and much more dangerous than any ghost you may encounter along the way.

Caves seem to be a repository for ghostly energies. Isolated caves were used for many enterprises during times past; during the Prohibition era, speakeasies were hidden deep inside caves. The KKK held secluded meetings in caves to avoid being observed. It also goes without saying that many magical or occult groups used caves for their hidden meetings and rituals.

It would not be unusual to photograph a miner hard at work, figures wearing white sheets (not to be confused with a ghost), or any number of eerie forms or apparitions in a cave. Magical or occult events certainly manifest anomalies, unlike the traditional ghosts or residual energy that you might encounter as a ghost hunter or paranormal investigator. Again, if you do not feel confident to investigate these unseen energies, leave them alone.

Old mines and mine shafts could also harbor the ghosts of miners who lost their lives while working there, trapping their energy much as they were trapped. Old mines often collapsed, and many times those buried deep inside were never recovered. New shafts were opened and the old ones were sealed with the bodies inside so that work could be resumed. Old mines can be very eerie and also contain odd energies. They are extremely dangerous so *never* investigate them alone.

Tunnels and covered bridges seem to have extraordinary histories of ghostly activities. Many reported ghost sightings are at covered bridges and in tunnels. Why is this? It's possible that ghosts prefer the seclusion that these places can provide. Perhaps they are the sites of automobile accidents, murders, or suicides. No matter the reason, these are excellent sources to include in your field trips and vacations. Who knows what you might record or photograph?

NOTE: In regard to caves, mines, and entryways that lead underground, be extremely careful. There are some who believe that there is an entire hidden civilization underground, deep within the earth. They may not look like us and, indeed, may be alien to us.

HISTORICAL HOMES

A house is a house is a house. Hardly! Throughout history, houses have been used as more than just residences. They have also been used for secretly hidden or otherwise concealed activities. Some archaic old houses often played host to decades and even centuries of ghostly activity.

One such covert activity was the now famous Underground Railroad. The Underground Railroad was a vast network of people who helped fugitive slaves escape to the North and Canada during the Civil War. It was not run by any single organization or person, but rather it consisted of many individuals and numerous homes. The homes and businesses where the fugitives could rest and eat were called "stations" and "depots" and were run by "stationmasters." For the slave, running away was anything but easy. The first step, of course, was to escape. The fugitives moved at night and traveled from station to station where they could stop and rest, hiding in out-of-the way places. Such places were often hidden in homes as secret rooms, crawl spaces, basements, root cellars, and attics. Countless fugitives arrived at the stations mortally injured, ill, and mentally exhausted. Many did not survive their trek toward safety. The people who aided and abetted them often buried the fugitives in secluded areas where their bodies would stay hidden. These secret burial grounds were usually on the homeowner's property, and it has been recorded that they even buried fugitives in their fields to guarantee that they would never be found. There have been many reported accounts of ghosts being seen in homes that were known to shelter the fugitives. Some of these old homes have been transformed from their former family status into homes for unwed mothers, orphanages, brothels, or businesses.

When researching an old mansion, it is almost mandatory that you learn the history of the house before you begin the investigation. This can be as simple or as detailed as you deem necessary, but you should include this research as an essential part of your investigation. These stately old homes may have survived wars, fires, floods, and storms, which tells me that they have very protective spirits watching over them. I always get excited at the prospect of investigating fantastic old homes from bygone eras. They have stories to share and ghosts to deliver their messages.

Any home for unwed mothers will have probably undergone extensive renovations to accommodate the needs of the young mothers. However, I am sure this does nothing to prevent paranormal activity from surfacing, especially if the renovators upset the ghosts. Upon investigation, you may get a sense of sadness and depression due to the previous occupants' state of affairs. However, I know for a fact that ghosts can be very protective of pregnant mothers and babies so you may encounter very benevolent ghosts while you are there. You may hear the sounds of babies crying as well as noise of the activities associated with the affairs of the house at that particular time.

Often these huge old houses were used as homes for abandoned or wayward children. These homes could be filled with childhood chatter, laughter, crying, and sounds of angry scuffles. The current homeowner may also hear feet running across the floors or up and down the stairs, balls bouncing off the floors and walls, and the sounds of children playing. All the noises of childhood may surface to greet an unsuspecting ghost hunter or new homeowner. When investigating, you may be able to photograph, video-tape, or capture a recording of a child who has passed over but chooses for whatever reason to stay at home. Children, as ghosts, are open and responsive to ghost hunters. They are also mischievous and curious. They usually represent no danger to the home owner and may eventually be a welcome guest, especially if the people who live there are childless or have a large family. You can almost always learn the child's name while you are investigating the home. They will want you to know it. As a child, their "name" is their all-encompassing identity.

Ghost hunters are often called to a home to investigate because a child is being frightened by a ghost. However, after the initial interview you may find that it is the parents who are terrified, not the children. Ghosts seem to appear to children on a consistent basis. Not only do children interact with ghosts (without fear), they also see spirits, disembodied loved ones, and animal spirits.

The presence of children in the home seems to have a way of enticing a ghost out into the open; they will usually become more active or materialize to the children as imaginary playmates. This is usually confusing and alarming to parents, especially if they are plagued with other paranormal activities in the house.

During the early nineteenth century, fantastic homes were often turned into flamboyant "painted ladies" (literally). Some took on new personas as they became brothels and bordellos. After the saloons and barrooms closed, cowboys, gamblers, cattlemen, and hired hands would seek out "soiled doves" and "painted ladies" for comfort. Some houses were bawdy, loud, and boisterous, filled with piano players, drinking, dancing, and other activities that were very exciting! Other houses were upscale and very discreet, usually catering to the community's finest: politicians, sheriffs, deputies, bankers, shopkeepers, and lawyers.

What an array of energies these old houses must have accumulated! One can only guess at the activities that still exist in the realm of vibrational frequencies inaccessible to us—the dramas, the discreet rendezvous, and the passions of the past.

Do these old houses have ghosts? Are you kidding? How could they not! If you are a ghost hunter at a site such as this, you will probably hear all the sounds associated with a house of ill repute. You may hear glasses clinking, pianos playing, guitar music, giggling, and ghostly moans and groans. You could witness or be able to photograph a full flamboyant apparition dressed in a ball gown or in period dress. Male or female, it would be enchanting indeed to capture this on film. Perhaps you can record a discreet conversation or chatter filled with laughter. We have an upcoming investigation at a lovely three-story home that was once home to a bordello, and I for one can hardly wait!

Of course, as with life in general, there was always the darker side of reality. That reality was that women were often abused or worse and men were murdered. These stately older homes will probably reflect these images of life in the form of a ghost or apparition. So be prepared and, as always, expect the unexpected!

ISOLATED ROADS

Numerous reports abound about weary travelers who have happened upon a ghost standing in the middle of a road near a cemetery or abandoned building. And who hasn't heard stories of travelers giving someone a ride, only later to learn that the person they had picked up was a "ghost"!

The idea of investigating isolated stretches of roadway, train tracks, or bridges at first didn't appeal to me. That was before I photographed an amazing portal on an isolated country road near a bridge. It just goes to show that you never know what to expect when on an investigation or field trip.

Folklore is replete with tales of ghosts appearing to people stranded or stopped at a crossroads. My grandmother used to say that ghosts waited at crossroads for unsuspecting travelers. If they waited too long trying to make up their minds which way to go, the ghost would move inside them and give them a new direction in life. "Really!," I said, full of wonder and amazement. To this day, it is hard for me to stop completely at a crossroads!

Having given this a lot of thought for many years, I believe that it is possible that any place where two paths intersect or cross can become a portal. Directional vibrations can become intertwined and change the energy pattern, allowing ghosts and spirits to enter our dimension.

With this in mind, find a crossroads in the country and see what happens. Stand there or park there and see if your perception changes. Take pictures to see what is revealed. And you could also try to communicate with the ghosts who are waiting there. You could, but will you?

LIBRARIES

Guess what? Libraries are some of the most haunted places you will ever enter. It seems that ghosts really are drawn to the peaceful solitude of libraries. There are many different kinds of libraries: genealogy libraries, medical libraries, rare book libraries, historical libraries, and community libraries. Here in America we even have presidential libraries. They are enormous repositories of knowledge. Is that why ghosts inhabit them? Probably not, but nonetheless they are there, hiding in shadowy corners and between massive bookcases.

Even the energies in a library are different and unusual. They seem subtle and yet powerful. I haven't been able to photograph any ghosts or anomalies inside these establishments due to library restrictions, but I am not giving up. I am confident that someday I will be able to investigate an old or abandoned library.

Whether you are part of a team or investigating on your own, you will need examples. Where do they come from?

Hopefully I have given you a few ideas. Also remember that when you have nothing pending, put together a field trip as these are often rewarding as well as motivating.

As a last resort you can check out local genealogy societies, historical societies, or delve into newspapers from long ago. Most libraries have old newspapers on microfilm; you might find them extremely helpful in your research.

There are many more places than I have mentioned here, and you will develop an "ear" for statements regarding ghosts as you do more and more investigations. Ghosts can be found in the most unlikely places as well as traditional haunts. Follow all leads; there is no telling where they will lead you. Of course, I believe that it is spirit that directs us.

THREE

HAUNTED POSSESSIONS WITH GHOSTLY CONNECTIONS

Beware! Lest you become possessed; by my possessions!

M. R. G. Long (1948–)

How often have you bought an item for your home or yourself only to find that after a few hours or days you begin to feel uncomfortable with its presence? Have you suddenly regretted buying something? Perhaps a new acquisition makes you feel sad or you become overwhelmed with emotion. If this has happened to you, you are probably experiencing the essence of the previous owner; in fact, they may be standing right beside you. Their energy may or may not have passed over to another realm of existence.

Antique dealers, who frequently buy from estate sales, find that events such as these are often common occurrences. They discuss the fact that they were just drawn to a piece or just could not keep from touching an object. Another unique occurrence is when someone unpacks their purchases and they find an item they do not remember buying. How did it get there? Who put it there? Perhaps a ghost wanted that particular person to have that object for reasons known only to them, especially if it was a very valuable piece. Having worked in this field for many years, I have experienced this on many levels.

Many sensitive people experience waves of intuitive impressions while shopping in antique malls and shops that sell vintage antiques. While touching an item, they may be able to feel or sense the residual energy that has been stored in that object by its previous owner. This energy may cause an image or emotion to surface from seemingly nowhere. This may be due to the fact that there is a ghostly presence near them. While holding a rolling pin, they may get a sense of someone baking bread and the aroma may seem to float through the air, stirring memories deep within. They might pick up an antique shaving mug and get a sense of what the person who used it daily looked like; indeed, he may be touching it still. The examples are as varied and numerous as the antiques waiting to be sold. Antique shops are among the most haunted places I have found.

Dealers who buy for short-term profit may not feel the energy associated with an object. However, I have often heard dealers say, "I didn't buy anything because nothing seemed to catch my attention or nothing jumped out at me." Similarly, I have heard the opposite just as often. "It just seemed to leap off the shelf" or "I just couldn't leave it sitting there" or (and I am guilty of this) "I just couldn't help myself. I couldn't stop bidding!" Of course there is always my favorite: "It just spoke to me." Imagine that!

Have you ever wondered why you purchased something that didn't match anything else in your house? Why, out of a multitude of choices, you picked that particular item? While shopping, have you ever suddenly noticed something out of your peripheral vision and ended up taking it home? You were probably answering a summons from another dimension or realm of existence. Although these energy connections may be beyond our mortal understanding, I believe we should accept these bizarre events as messages from spirits or ghosts who are communicating with us. Perhaps these items were once their personal possessions and they wish to remain near them. Or perhaps they would rather see something that was dear to them in a particular house or with a special person, again for reasons known only to them.

One spring during a visit to upstate New York, I purchased a precious antique composition baby doll. She had the sweetest expression on her face, and I couldn't wait to get home and display her. I sat her in a vintage chair in our den; however, she didn't remain there for long. As family and friends came to visit, their first comment was often, "Where did you get that weird doll?" Well, I was shocked to say the least because I thought she was lovely. What were they seeing that I couldn't? My children had similar experiences; they referred to her as eerie, even saying that her eyes followed them around. Now, I'll have to admit that to hear my adult children say things like that was a little disconcerting for me. My precious doll! What on earth was going on?

Everyone began giving her a wide berth, even walking around the chair she sat in just to avoid her. One day my little granddaughter said, "NanNa, please take her away. She makes me scared!" Needless to say, she was on the auction block the following Saturday night. She sold for a ridiculously low price. However, I have never regretted the monetary loss, as the peace and harmony that returned to my house was well worth the loss. I wonder what others could see or feel that was beyond my intuition. She was so pretty, but was I only seeing what she wanted me to see? Were my family and friends sensing the previous owner? Was she with her favorite doll? A unique experience indeed! In all my years of antiquing, that was my only uncomfortable experience with possessions belonging to others.

As spiritual energy, we are always transforming and transmitting energy. We transform all forms of matter that we come into contact with. As pure energy, we are capable of interacting with the molecules of any solid matter, and we leave indelible evidence. We create imprints that can be sensed through psychic awareness, often presenting startling sights, sounds, and smells. As these energy imprints take on various forms, they may cause us to become emotional, which can be confusing, especially if we are not aware of the changes that ghosts are able to manifest.

Many religious disciplines dictate that we should live our lives as clutter-free as possible, that we should not be materially minded. The process of letting go becomes a constant reminder of our ability to control our lives. However, I believe that keeping things of sentimental value adds energy to our homes and our lives and ultimately brings us peace and comfort. Our most cherished knickknacks and collectibles are often common things that we endow with special meaning from past experiences. We remember the spiritual essence connected to these things and want to keep them close to us.

Objects as well as people bind us to others. Sometimes objects are kept secretly, like privately owned treasures in a vault, or they might be displayed to communicate affection. Many ghosts may retain a connection to personal items that were significant to them during the days when they were here. Powerful energies are associated with objects. These emotionally charged energies can be transmitted to an object and can remain within it for decades or even centuries.

The following story took place two years ago and is a good indication of how personal objects can become endowed with their previous owner's energy.

AGATHA'S GHOST AND HER CRYSTAL BALL

One warm summer day I decided to go antiquing with my daughter and a friend of ours. We spent most of the day hitting one garage sale after another looking for treasures. We also stopped at the local flea market to browse for things we just couldn't live without. Before we called it a day, we decided to stop in and say hello to Peggy Hawkins, an antique dealer who has a unique knack for finding odd, unusual, and sometimes very different things. Her shop, "Needful Things," is filled to the brim with a variety of antiques and collectibles.

She asked me if I was still interested in the metaphysical arts and the occult, and of course my ears perked up! I answered that I was and probably always would be. She said that she had something she wanted to show me. She went behind a big ornate walnut showcase and pulled out a very large crystal ball. I was astounded at its size, as well as its obvious age. She asked me if I could feel anything by holding it. Now I was really intrigued!

"Why?" I asked. "Just try it," she replied. I held the heavy crystal ball in my hands and immediately it began to feel warmer. This was unusual, as crystal almost always remains cool to the touch. I sensed a familiarity with the ball but couldn't quite discern what I was feeling. She watched me closely as if expecting something to happen. When I did not produce the result she obviously expected, she said, "Sit down, I want to tell you a story."

She related to us that another antique dealer had purchased a cannonball (or so it seemed) from someone who had found it buried several feet underground. It was unearthed beneath an old house that was well over 150 years old at the time it was torn down.

The dealer brought the cannonball to her for identification, as she was familiar with Civil War artifacts. As she began the task of cleaning it up, her curiosity increased dramatically. Evidently the ball had become encased in soil and minerals over a long period of time and had acquired the appearance of a cannonball. Upon closer investigation, it appeared to be wrapped in cheesecloth or a similar material. As she cleaned it with a steel brush, pieces began to chip away and, much to her amazement, a crystal ball was revealed. It was perfectly spherical in shape, with no scratches, nicks, or noticeable damage. She polished it to a brilliant sheen. She then called the dealer and asked him to come over and see what she had found. He rushed right over to see for himself what she had uncovered. Of course he was very pleased and thanked her accordingly.

However, the excitement he had with his new acquisition was short-lived. He began to have problems with his marriage, and perhaps looking for an outside source on which to place the blame, he readily attributed his misfortune to the crystal ball. He called Peggy once again and offered to sell her the crystal ball. As she already had a vested interest in the ball, she offered to trade with him for some collectibles. Of course she did not believe his story and felt he was only seeking monetary gain.

Finding the crystal ball very interesting, Peggy's son asked her if he could have it. He took it home and kept it for six months, displaying it on his coffee table. During that time he suffered two failed relationships. He also broke his leg in two places and some of his guns were stolen, as well as two automobiles. And as if this weren't enough to add to his mounting problems, he was also shot in the eye with a BB gun. To avoid even more problems, he returned the crystal ball to his mother's shop in the hope that his problems would end. Strangely enough, they did.

After a short time, a man came into the shop and asked about the crystal ball, which he found prominently displayed on top of an antique showcase. Wanting to purchase it, he asked her for her best price. She had no qualms about pricing it at $200, and after haggling over the price, the sale was completed.

Shortly thereafter, the man's luck changed. He lost his job where he had worked for over thirty years, his wife left him, and he became seriously ill. He also had two car wrecks, which left him confused and unsettled to say the least. Depressed and unhappy, he returned the crystal ball to Peggy and asked her to please buy it back. Feeling somewhat responsible, she refunded his money and took the ball back into her shop.

Before long, another man offered to buy the unique crystal sphere. Feeling that she must reveal the truth about the ball, she related the stories of the other men who had purchased it. However, it didn't seem to bother this customer and another sale was made. It did not take long, however, before she heard of his bad luck. He lost the car dealership that he owned, and his wife left him. Although they eventually got back together, he had to be treated for depression and suffered severe anxiety attacks. He also began a new business but, in due time, he also lost that business. Frustrated and despondent, he returned the crystal ball, giving it back to Peggy with no thought of compensation. After returning the ball, he regained his health and his mental outlook vastly improved.

By now Peggy had decided not to sell the crystal ball ever again to a man. She was beginning to wonder about the crystal ball and its supposed power to wreak havoc on the lives of the men who bought it. She had never experienced any ill effects from having it in her shop, so she was puzzled as to why the men who bought it suffered such tragedies. In fact, she often played with the ball and seemed to have developed a connection with it. She would place it on her desk, and, as she moved her hands from left to right, the ball would follow her hands back and forth across the surface of the desk. This began to scare her! She placed it back in the showcase and never attempted to use it again.

As fate would have it, another man ventured into her shop and noticed the crystal ball sitting in the showcase. When he asked about it, Peggy of course related all the stories to him. He laughed wholeheartedly and said, "Hand me that ball. I'm not afraid of it and to prove it to you, I'll buy it right now!" He continued to make fun of his new acquisition, saying he didn't believe in hexes of any kind. He continued to laugh as he left the shop; his laughter, however, was short-lived. Within a few months, he suffered the same fate as the other men before him. He suddenly developed heart problems that eventually led to three heart surgeries. His wife left him, and he developed a severe sexual dysfunction that was devastating to him. Frustrated and despondent, he returned the crystal ball as soon as he was able. While in the shop he purchased a lovely Victorian cross to wear. He later told Peggy that his problems ceased to exist as soon as he returned the ball; he regained his health and his mental outlook was vastly improved.

After this last encounter, Peggy decided again to never sell the crystal ball to a man. She would not even allow a man to touch it. Although she has never experienced any ill effects from this unique sphere, she is convinced that there may be negative energy attached to it that is directed toward any man who touches it.

I left her shop enthralled by her stories and very curious about the crystal ball. What an amazing story! Little did I know that the rest of the story was on the way! I had just settled down in my recliner to rest after the long day of antiquing when I heard a faint whisper in my right ear. As I am clairvoyant as well as clairaudient, I was not surprised to hear the feminine voice that demanded my attention. This often happens when I am overly tired or emotionally drained. As I began to relax to accommodate her frequency of communication, she said, "Listen and I will tell you the truth about the crystal ball." Thinking the voice would say that the stories I had just heard about the crystal ball were a sham, I reluctantly allowed her to continue. Here is her story as she related it to me verbatim. I am leaving nothing out of, nor adding anything to, her narrative.

"My name is Agatha," she said. "A terrible tragedy afflicted me in 1901 when I was but twenty years old. I was busying myself with my needlepoint in the parlor when suddenly I sensed someone in the room. The dark shadows hid someone's presence, a man, and I was puzzled as to why he was there. He was older than I, and his large frame overpowered mine. I recognized him as an associate of my father who had requested my hand in marriage. Much to my father's displeasure, I had turned down his proposal. 'Sir, why have you come here?' I asked as I stood to meet his gaze in defiance. I told him that I would never marry him and that his money would never lay claim to me.

"Enraged, he grabbed my arms. I jerked away and slapped him soundly on the cheek. He threw me down on the floor and pinned me there with his arms. He declared that although he might never wed me, I would be defiled for any future promise of happiness. I endured the rape as an ocean of tears flooded my face. I never uttered a word as the deed was carried out. He arose and left me lying there, battered and bruised. As he sat in a chair strapping up his boots, I got up from the floor. I grabbed a crystal ball that rested on the mantel and slipped up behind him. I slammed it into his head. He slumped forward in the chair, never to breathe again. I took a deep breath as I avenged my soul.

This ball is witness to the death of thee.
No man shall ever again do harm to me!
To all men who touch and all who see,
Devastation shall come to thee!

"I walked out to the barn and got a huge cotton-picking sack with a large shoulder strap. I took it into the house, pulled his body into it, and dragged him into the yard. I stood there for the longest time, warming my soul in the setting sun. Suddenly, a light breeze gave me notice that it was time to complete my task. I dragged him into the root cellar behind a giant chinaberry tree at the rear of the house. There I dumped his body into a cold, damp grave.

"I returned to the house and went back into the parlor. I looked for the crystal ball and lifted it up to the window. How could such a lovely crystal sphere become a weapon? Nevertheless, its beauty remained a constant reminder of my pain and heartache. I took the ball down to the cellar and buried it very deep in the soft ground so it would remain secreted away from my memory.

Because your heart is pure and true,
Many blessings will come to you.
On this day as you witness my story through,
This ball of truth I give to you.
You will prosper and grow and more.
Peace and love shall come to your door.
I must go now…Agatha…Agatha."

As Agatha's voice drifted away, I sat there in total silence. Images of her life raced through my mind, and my heart was filled with sadness. I felt like I was caught up in an emotional whirlwind. What was my connection to her, to the crystal ball? Were we connected in a past life? Will I ever know the answers? Should I buy the crystal ball? What would happen if I did?

The crystal ball rested quietly for the last two years in the same shop where I first held it. As a matter of fact, I was the last person to touch it or hold it. Guess what? I recently received it as a gift from a very dear friend, and it now sits in a locked case in my house. Perhaps Agatha will return and make her wishes known to me or maybe she is content now that her confession is out. Could it be that now that her secret is out she is happy for the crystal ball to rest where it is? Only time will tell. This experience with Agatha's ghost has been very emotional for me, but I would not have missed it for anything.

GHOSTLY MESSAGES

Ghosts use objects to communicate and deliver messages. In this sense, objects may become carriers of psychic content. They may express the ghost's desire to communicate by linking matter and spirit. The objects become finely attuned to the ghost's energy with startling results and may retain a connection for generations to come. Ghosts may retain a connection to jewelry, furniture, heirlooms, toys, mirrors, and portraits, to name a few. Books, curios, clocks, lamps, and music boxes may all become messengers for ghosts. Mechanical objects are favorites for ghosts as they are easy to manipulate and use as forms of communication.

Our ancestors were well aware of the fact that energy enhanced matter. Soldiers never left home for a battle without carrying with them a remembrance of their loved ones. A photograph, a scarf, or a letter—something they could touch with their soul that would bring them peace and comfort and perhaps protection. There are many accounts of soldiers dying during the Civil War and something belonging to them suddenly showing up in their home. This was, without a doubt, a gift from another realm of existence.

Whenever you touch something, you leave little particles of yourself behind as microscopic samples of your DNA and genetic coding. Every object you handle retains some of your energy. Some things retain energy impressions longer than others due to the density of their matter. Silver and gold objects—such as keys, lockets, and jewelry with diamonds and precious gemstones—may hold someone's energy for generations. Energy may also be held for long periods of time in fabrics and paper, especially if the paper and ink have been emotionally charged, as in a love letter, for example. Perhaps the energy is retained for the future and secreted away until the message is energized and shared with the person for whom it was intended. If this is the case, a ghost will direct someone to it.

Ghosts are able to create emotional vignettes for the soul. In touching an object, you may sense joy or a great sadness, peace and contentment, or simply pleasure and spiritual understanding. In your mind's eye, you may glimpse images of another era and intuitively realize that you were part of that time and place. The stronger the emotion connected to an object, the more vivid the ghost's presence may be sensed. This event may lead to actually seeing the apparition or ghost that is producing the phenomena.

Have you ever gazed deeply into an antique mirror and for a split second sensed another person looking back at you? Beautiful, ornate mirrors can transport you to another dimensional reality. They reflect images from the past as well as the present. Ghosts use mirrors as forms of communication. They appear easily in them and often display symbols in an attempt to get their messages across. Watch closely for any symbol that may appear. These are messages in and of themselves. Ghosts who have transformed to a higher vibrational frequency often use symbols to trigger memories that will assure, beyond a shadow of a doubt, that they are there.

Gently gazing into a mirror transforms your vibrational frequency and alters your perception of time and space, creating a portal to other realms of existence. When you see yourself in a mirror, you are actually seeing yourself simultaneously in the past, present, and future. Although all you may see is your immediate image, you exist on three distinctly separate vibrational levels. As you transcend time and space, one image will gain prominence over the others. This can be very exciting and even confusing as you are never quite sure of what you will see or who will appear.

As you transcend the barriers of time and space, you will notice that the mirror's glass may become wavy or that small orb-shaped bubbles may seem to float freely in the glass. The glass may take on a shimmering effect and actually sparkle. These are all indications of the presence of ghostly energy. If the previous owner was attached to the mirror or if it was perhaps their favorite, you may catch a glimpse of them looking back at you. Often, friends and relatives who have died will appear as ghosts to convey messages. These images may be fleeting at first. However, should you experience this form of ghostly contact, you may wish to use your mirror as a way of communicating with ghosts in other dimensions. If so, the images will appear for longer periods of time, and you will gain confidence as the communication improves with time.

Ghosts present themselves to us in a variety of ways. As I am primarily clairaudient, I hear them more than I see them. The following story is a clear indication of how I interact with ghosts and how they sometimes interact with me.

I attended an estate auction in an old barn and was surprised to find a quilt in such an unlikely place. It was tucked inside a weathered toolbox. Dusty and weary from years of use, it finally came to rest on the auction block. It wasn't particularly pretty and had no apparent pattern or design to speak of, but I was really drawn to that well-worn quilt. As the auctioneer held up the gigantic dust rag, my hand flew up, seemingly of its own volition. My husband looked at me as if I had lost my mind. There were few women at the auction so the bidding was sparse, but I just couldn't seem to control my bidding paddle. Needless to say, in less time than it takes to spell *quilt*, I was the proud owner of that piece of art. One look from my husband told me that I couldn't bring it into the house, so I tossed it rather unceremoniously over the back of a rocker on the front porch. Days passed, and I couldn't quite seem to pass that quilt without it calling out to me. Well, what was I going to do with it? My husband offered to burn it! Had he lost his mind? Evidently! As I sat on the porch with the quilt across my lap pondering what I was going to do with it, my eyes were drawn to a faded quilt block. As I looked at the threadbare block, I thought I could see a hint of a deep rose color inside the quilt. Yes it was! "Oh, my gosh!" I exclaimed. "This quilt has another quilt inside of it."

Remembering stories of how often a new quilt top and lining were added to an old quilt to preserve it, I became very excited. Now I had the answer to my question, and I began to snip the long stitches that held it all together. While I was snipping away, a cool breeze started swirling all around me. I felt goose bumps on the back of my neck. I was fully aware that there was a ghost nearby. Then I heard a very gentle voice say "Thank you." I felt a little silly as I replied "You're welcome." As more and more of the quilt was exposed, I sensed the quilt maker standing near me. Before long I had uncovered a worn, but absolutely beautiful, delicate Lone Star patterned quilt. It was lovely, and it was obvious that much love and care had gone into choosing the pieces, as they complemented each other perfectly. The stitches were tiny and precise—the mark of a master quilt maker. Hidden discreetly in one corner were embroidered these words: "When this you see, remember me." Although I do not know her name, I will always sense her, and she will definitely be remembered with spiritual understanding. The quilt must have been very special to her because she made sure that it survived the ravages of time. I still have this quilt and cherish it as a gift crafted from unseen hands.

Books are interesting examples of things that ghosts use to get our attention. Books are powerful forms of communication and more often than not are inspired from the spiritual realm. When you are attracted to a book of any kind for whatever reason, it is to enhance your spiritual understanding of vibrational frequencies and alternate realities.

Books will contribute to your soul's energy by empowering you emotionally, psychologically, and spiritually. The very reason you are drawn to a book is a distinct indication of your relationship to the knowledge and wisdom contained within.

Have you ever entered a bookstore to buy a specific book only to leave with an entirely different book, perhaps on a completely different subject? Have you ever been searching for a book in a bookstore and had one fall off the shelf right in front of you? And if so, when picking it up did you find that it held precisely the information you were looking for? Are you drawn to old books that just feel good, look interesting, or seem special for some unknown reason? If you have experienced any of these events, you have been the recipient of ghostly contact. Someone is trying to communicate with you, and books are a convenient way of making their presence known.

Books often reveal mysterious hidden messages for you and you alone. You may purchase a book and not read it for days or even years. You will read what you need to know when it is time to enhance your spirituality or begin a new growth pattern. You may read an entire book, a few pages, or only one sentence. However, you have read exactly the message you were meant to receive, and it was probably someone dear to you (albeit in ghostly form) who directed you to it.

Clocks are occult "keepers of time." Vintage, delicately carved timepieces may span generations of time and space. In centuries past, not everyone owned ornate furniture or priceless dinnerware, but everyone had a clock.

Clocks are mysterious regulators of energy. How often do you glance at a clock, your wristwatch, or a pocket watch? How different our lives would be without these timely devices! Superstition tells us that it is bad luck to have more than one clock in the same room at the same time. However, in today's society we are surrounded with constant reminders of time.

Ghosts find mechanical objects easy to manipulate for contact and will often use clocks as a primary source of communication. Clocks have been known to stop at the exact time of someone's death, never to work again. Often, alarm clocks will go off at the exact hour of a relative's death, just to let you know that they are safe and happy in their new dimensional frequency. If you awaken at a particular time of night on several repeated occasions, someone is trying to get a message to you. Always take note of the exact time, as this in itself may be a message to be discerned through numerology.

Numerology and clocks, as well as time, are closely related. The word *clock* indicates knowledge of spiritual matters, just as the word *time* indicates psychic communication. Ghosts may use timepieces to communicate or clarify messages. Be open and receptive to anything going on when you are awakened. Ghosts may use your clock as a catalyst to "wake you up"—literally! Some clocks chime on the hour. Be aware that this sets up a vibration within your house that may be conducive to ghostly contact.

Clocks come in many shapes, sizes, and styles. You may be drawn to antique clocks such as mantel clocks, carriage clocks, pocket watches, or grandfather clocks. These clocks have a special allure and have been strongly imprinted by their previous owners. They were handled daily due to the fact that they needed to be wound repeatedly. These old clocks are often haunted by their former owners as well as the original clockmakers who could have become attached to their works of art.

Ghosts want to communicate with us. Loved ones who have gone ahead of us want us to know that they are happy. They will frequently use anything mechanical to get our attention. Chimes may jingle without the presence of wind to stir them. Televisions and radios may turn off and on repeatedly, and your telephone may ring at the exact time that someone passes over. You may answer your phone and hear the voice of your deceased loved one on the other end. If you experience these things, you're not crazy and you do not have an overactive imagination. No, it is not just wishful thinking either. You are being contacted by a ghost!

For me, there is a strong spiritual awareness that emerges after years of hearing and seeing ghosts. My own personal knowledge of paranormal phenomena has proven that ghosts do return again and again to be near loved ones as well as favorite things they were forced to leave behind.

FOUR

A GHOSTLY PRESENCE

*It is the secret of the world that all things subsist
and do not die, but retire a little from sight and afterwards
return again. Nothing is dead. People feign themselves dead,
and endure mock funerals and mournful obituaries,
and there they stand, looking out of the window,
sound and well in some new disguise.*

RALPH WALDO EMERSON (1803–1882)

The word *ghost* is a widely misused, catch-all term for all types of paranormal activities, some of which have absolutely nothing to do with ghosts at all. The idea of ghosts as disembodied souls has been around throughout the history of humanity. No matter what we believe or disbelieve today, it was probably perceived the exact same way hundreds of years ago. There will always be those of us who believe, as well as those who remain skeptical disbelievers.

I do not always find ghosts. They find me! I believe that most of the people who have an uncanny experience with ghosts are themselves clairvoyant to a certain degree and therefore capable of being able to communicate with discarnate energies such as ghosts and spirits. There is nothing mysterious, occult, or magical about our innate spiritual gifts. These unique gifts are part of our spiritual inheritance and will allow us to experience other dimensional frequencies such as ghosts and extraordinary paranormal phenomena.

Ghosts have the ability to contact us through our senses, including our unique sixth sense. Telepathy and intuition are among some of our most prominent gifts and should be acknowledged as such, along with the other gifts of clairvoyance and clairaudience.

In their attempts to make contact, ghosts may make dramatic appearances that can send chills up and down your spine. They may also appear in your dreams. This is a common occurrence although most people are not aware of it. As ghosts, they have the ability to communicate with us through a combination of all of our senses.

So what exactly is a ghost? They are people who have been unable or unwilling to make the transition from their physical state into the world of spirit, from our dimensional frequency to the next. The people who do not make this transition may be anchored by the circumstances of their deaths. They may not have been able to reconcile the fact that they are no longer within the physical realm of existence.

Throughout time, man has sought to understand death giving rise to spirits. The more we understand death, the less we will fear our own transition and the easier it will become to relate to ghosts as "invisible people." Most people are reluctant to talk about death and usually avoid it at all costs, so it's no wonder that they are afraid of ghosts.

Our physical body exists due to the electrical impulses that keep it energized—the essence of our soul. When we die (for lack of a better word), we stop breathing and everything that was energized by the electrical charges in our bodies ceases to function. End of story? Not necessarily. These electrical impulses have to go somewhere. But where do they go? They are transformed into another form. Since energy can't be destroyed, it becomes a new (glorified) form, either spirit or ghosts depending upon one's level of spiritual awareness. This new electromagnetic form is capable of direct communication and interaction with us. They are merely operating through a finer vibrational frequency than they were before.

The most common form of death is, of course, the transition from the physical body to the spirit body without difficulty, and without feeling the need to stay in the dense physical atmosphere of the earth. The majority of souls embrace this transition, thus becoming "free spirits." As such they are capable of communicating with us according to their desire, intent, and ability to adjust to their new state of being.

However, for many people, although death has freed them from their physical bodies, their lack of spiritual understanding still confines them to their past earthly existence. A person may have experienced a shock so severe that a normal transition was impossible. Murders, unexpected accidents, suicides, and even sudden deaths can keep ghosts earthbound. When murder and crimes of passion are involved, a ghost may remain because of the need to correct an injustice or out of anger or possibly even vengeance. They may want to solve the mystery of their death. Often they will relate messages regarding their deaths that will ultimately solve the crime.

When these events unfold, the ghosts are probably not aware of their true state of being. They may not be able to comprehend their distorted reality. They do not know they are dead, but they may realize they are not quite the way they were before. After all, our bodies are just vibrational illusions. How easily we could transition from one dimension to the next if we could only grasp the concept of vibrations and frequencies as true reality! A ghost is merely a manifestation of transformed spiritual energy.

When we perceive ghosts either visually or audibly, we are interacting with them because the event could not take place without two active participants. They see us and we see them because the desire and intent is there, either consciously or unconsciously, or possibly both.

I get so tickled at some of my ghost-hunting buddies, because they profess that they really want to have a ghostly experience and yet, on the other hand, they are saying, "Oh my, what will we do if we see a ghost?" They are setting up a confusing atmosphere for themselves as well as any ghost that may be considering contact.

When we experience paranormal phenomena or see a ghost, we do so because they are resonating to our vibrational frequency. We do *not* see a ghost by accident! They either want us to see them or they don't, and there is not a lot we can do to encourage them if they are not willing to communicate with us. We are able to detect them with our equipment only because they allow us to. I firmly believe this. Here's an example of what I mean.

One morning as I was taking the kids to school, I stopped to fill my car up with gas. While I was there I was fortunate to see a very genteel ghost.

The car next to mine was being fueled by a man who looked to be about sixty years old. Inside his shiny new car sat a very lovely, older, gray-haired woman who appeared to be at least eighty years old. She was staring straight ahead and never glanced to either the left or the right. As I watched her I noticed how out of place she appeared. I noticed several unusual things about her. She was dressed in clothes from a much earlier era. Her silver hair was pulled back in a bun, and she had a soft glow about her. In her hands she held a beautiful porcelain teacup and saucer. Her cup and saucer were so delicate that I could see the sun sparkle through them. They were decorated with tiny delicate purple pansies, a favorite flower of mine. I remember thinking how oddly she was dressed and how unusual it was for her to be sitting there in that car, sipping tea, that early in the morning. She held her teacup so daintily that she almost seemed to be a mannequin.

When the man returned after paying for his gas, he got in his fancy car and started his engine, never even glancing toward the woman who sat there beside him. She never moved or acknowledged him either. She remained as still as a statue. Even her teacup was still held in the exact position as when I first noticed her. I knew I was staring but I simply could not take my eyes off of them.

Then as he drove away, the woman turned ever so slightly to look at me, and I saw the faintest smile creep across her face. I caught a glimpse of a very lovely pink cameo on the neck of her dress (cameos are very special to me, too.) Then, and only then, did I realize that she was a ghostly apparition.

The man drove away oblivious to his unseen passenger! I have always wondered if perhaps she was his mother or grandmother. Either way I am sure her presence was comforting to him in some way. Why did she allow me to see her? Well, I believe she was a messenger and the message was "Slow down and enjoy the simple things in life, like a warm cup of tea in the daintiest of teacups." By the way, if you haven't guessed it by now, the kids were late for school!

There are no chance meetings in our universe, and seeing a ghost is usually a well-orchestrated event for our benefit. Ghosts may appear spontaneously and then suddenly dissipate before our very eyes. They may appear transparent, solid, as full or partial apparitions, and may be dressed in clothes from another era as well as in modern everyday attire. It is extremely rare for a ghost to appear in the clothes they were buried in.

Ghosts must make adjustments in their vibrational frequency in order to become visible to us. We as humans are made up of dense vibrational matter. The faster that matter vibrates the less dense it becomes.

NOTE: At the time of death, we vibrate at such an accelerated rate of speed that we literally vibrate right out of our bodies, and we are instantly with our families, friends, and loved ones in the next highest frequency.

Ghosts exist at a higher vibrational frequency than we do as humans. In order to become visible to us, they must lower their vibrations. When these two vibrational forms (we are dense matter and ghosts are light matter) meet, contact is possible. This is one reason that visitations and encounters are often short and, dare I say, sweet. It is very hard for a ghost to maintain constant visibility because it has to gather and sustain enough energy to maintain an equal vibrational frequency—in other words, vibrate at our frequency.

This is also why most people see a ghost or spirit when they are emotionally distraught or extremely tired and perhaps emotionally exhausted. They are vibrating at a different frequency. During stressful situations and times of extreme duress, many people experience voices and apparitions. When people see deathbed apparitions, they are not hallucinating and it is not the effects of medications. They are seeing people in the room because *they are there.* Their vibrations have reached an apex, thereby opening a portal that allows them to see and hear from those who exist in other dimensions.

CRISIS GHOSTS

Crisis ghosts or apparitions appear to loved ones or close friends just seconds before their deaths and immediately thereafter. This is a very common ghost sighting, and while extremely heartbreaking it can also be emotionally healing. These sightings are more prominent during wartime and whenever great numbers of people die in catastrophic events such as earthquakes, floods, fires, or hurricanes.

Crisis ghosts appear to express their eternal love, to fulfill a promise to help ease the pain of grief, or simply to say a final goodbye.

When I said that an event like this could be heartbreaking, I should have added very traumatic as well. My father passed away rather suddenly and unexpectedly. I awoke early one morning to see my bedroom filled with light. My father was standing there just as real as he was the last time I saw him, which was only a few days before. He was speaking to me but I was too shocked to utter a word. My heart was beating so fast that I thought it would explode at any moment. He said, "Stop crying. I will be back in four years!" Then he was gone! I was left there in the darkness that replaced the light of his presence as my heart catapulted through the entire scope of emotions. Overwhelmed with great sadness, I moved from shock to puzzlement and finally came to rest with the peace that comes from understanding. Although this was without a doubt one of the most shocking events of my life, it was also one of the most empowering. I know beyond a shadow of a doubt that we do not die, we can and do come back to communicate with our loved ones, and I know that life and death are two sides of the same coin.

As for the statement my father made about returning in four years, my belief in reincarnation has been given a new foundation of truth. But wait, that is another book.

Ghosts are intelligent energy forms that contain the personality of the person who has been transformed. Just because a person dies does not mean that they will necessarily be different: better, holier, or sweeter, for that matter. If they were mean-spirited in life, they may remain so until they accept their new state of being and gravitate toward higher dimensions. If they were mischievous or a practical joker in life, you can almost count on them being one of those ghosts who will scare you silly—just for the fun of it. If they were loud, boisterous, and bold, their appearances will probably be very dramatic. If they were shy and reserved in life, they will be the ones who may touch you ever so lightly, make your hair stand up, or whisper in your ear. What they are really doing is finding a way to say, "I am right here. Please notice me."

As a ghost hunter or paranormal investigator, you may encounter all kinds of ghosts, from gentle and elusive to demanding and seemingly negative. Although to encounter a very angry or very negative ghost is rare, it may happen. So I really can't express this strongly enough: always expect the unexpected.

It seems that a majority of ghost sightings are documented as occurring between the hours of one and three AM. Electromagnetic energies are fluctuating at their thinnest vibrational frequency in the early morning hours and this allows for an easier transition of energies to other dimensions at the time of death. I have a ghost-hunting friend who always wants to stay out until after one in the morning, saying "I never get anything until after one AM." So maybe she is on to something.

Recognition is obviously a key factor in ghostly appearances. Although they may be recognized, their age and appearance may reflect another period in time rather than how we remember them. This was shown to my daughter in a most interesting way.

Tamatha, who was thirty-five years old at the time, was preparing for her daughter's graduation and totally immersed in her plans, when suddenly my father's ghost appeared before her. He had with him a young boy who appeared to be about six years old. My daughter and father engaged in conversation about our family. Apparently she was much more spiritually aware at that age than I was, and she was able to acknowledge him lovingly and spiritually. At one point she asked him who the little boy was. He replied, "This is my son. You have never seen him because he died before you were born." This was news to her because she didn't know about my younger brother. She asked me about it and I confirmed that it was indeed true ,and I told her that he had died when I was twelve. It's interesting that my daughter learned of her uncle, who passed away soon after his birth, from her deceased grandfather.

The event was an unexpected gift to my entire family. My mother was especially touched by it. There are not enough words to describe the joy and peace of mind she received from knowing that her late husband was caring for their beloved baby. Although my father was elderly when he died, he was able to appear younger to Tamatha and my brother appeared older, not as a baby. I believe the message was for my mother although it came through my daughter. I believe many messages from beyond the veil of illusion are delivered in much the same way every day.

From that experience, I learned that ghosts are able to project themselves to us just as they want us to see them. They create the atmosphere of their surroundings. They impress upon our senses what we need to feel, see, smell, or hear to understand them and their reason for contact.

Many times ghosts are earthbound by love. Ghost hunters and investigators may come across a haunting in which an individual or entire family may be keeping their loved one from moving on. They may be so obsessed with the departed soul that the ghost feels trapped and simply cannot make the transition to a new dimension. This situation would present a challenge for any ghost hunter. First of all, you will probably be faced with a genuine haunting. Second, the homeowner or client will probably not be open to surrendering their emotions and allowing the ghost to move on. In a case such as this, it's better left to a professional psychologist; you may have to bow out gracefully.

Ghosts may appear as solid as you and me. In this case they possess tremendous energy and will be very powerful. They may project an awesome and unforgettable presence. We were fortunate enough to capture such an image on film during an investigation in a huge abandoned train station that had been built back in 1929. We were on a return visit for further documentation when the full apparition was photographed. After about six hours of investigating, we were winding down. It had been a very rewarding site, and we were able to document a number of paranormal anomalies, including lots of orbs and streaming forms of energy. Perhaps an hour or so before we left, my daughter and I walked past an area that was once a concession stand in the early days of the station. It had since been remodeled many times with the last renovation being a bar; there was a private club there before it closed permanently.

As we walked by my daughter said, "Mom, I feel something over there." So we stood there and discussed her feelings, and then we both took several pictures in that direction. The next day while viewing our pictures on the computer, I was surprised and elated to see that a figure showed up in one of her pictures. He looks as real and solid as anyone you've ever seen. When the picture was magnified as much as possible, it became increasingly clear that she had captured a full apparition. It just does not get any better than this, unless of course it is on your own camera!

There were seven of us on our team that night, five women and two men. One of the men wore his cowboy hat and the other had a cap on. This really helped us to validate the fact that the apparition could not have been either one of them.

He appears to be wearing a visor of some sort, perhaps like men used to wear when working as clerks in the train station. He appears to be watching my daughter intently. We were all intrigued by his intense gaze. Did we draw him in? Has he always been there? Did he have a message for us? Are we going back to find out? You bet!

Ghost hunting is an intriguing, fun, exciting experience. To document a ghost or an apparition is a powerful event and one that most ghost hunters and investigators will never forget. Knowledge is power, and the best way to fight fear of the unknown is by exploring our ever-changing reality. We are all here to learn and enhance our spirituality and what better way than by exploring mysterious realms and ghostly phenomena as a ghost hunter or paranormal investigator.

FIVE

APPEARANCES OF
RESIDUAL GHOSTS

A memory is what is left when something happens
and does not completely unhappen.

EDWARD DE BONO (1960–)

When is a ghost not a ghost? When its residual energy is so strong that it leaves a lasting impression on the electro-magnetic vibrational field of its surroundings. These surroundings may be a house or a building of any kind, but it is not limited to structures. It has no boundaries and can manifest in open fields, parks, cemeteries, battlefields, or at crime scenes.

A residual haunting, like a ghost, is a complex phenom-enon and can be confusing even to the most experienced ghost hunter or paranormal investigator. Because its charac-teristics are so similar to those of a traditional ghost, people will often attribute it to a ghostly manifestation. In order to discern this particular type of paranormal manifestation, it's necessary to take all the combined activities generated by these phenomena and analyze them separately. There is always the off chance that there could be two or more differ-ent kinds of paranormal phenomena. It is not uncommon to document ecto-mist and orbs at the site of a residual ghost. This is a clear indication that much more is going on and will need to be investigated as a part of the whole.

After the initial shock of seeing an apparition, perhaps the first thing a client or homeowner will notice is that the ghost seems to be unaware of their presence. It may appear oblivious to the fact that it is in someone else's home and invading their space. It usually appears to be going about its personal business paying no attention to the startled witness.

These scenes usually unfold as if watching a movie. They may begin suddenly and end just as abruptly, as if someone had started a movie in the middle and then stopped it before the ending. This is a key element to residual haunting; it plays and replays, much as a movie in a VCR—start, stop, pause, and rewind, only to play the same scene again.

The participants appear to be caught unawares in scenarios that keep repeating themselves over and over again. These repeated scenes may replay daily, weekly, yearly, or only on anniversaries of some historical event known only to the ghost. They may be played and replayed for decades or centuries with no one there. These images are left from traumatic or emotionally significant events.

They may also be simply routine day-to-day life situations. Some scenes may be happy and others may be traumatic or downright frightening. However, it is important to remember that there is not anything associated with this haunting that can harm you.

You may witness crime scenes, murders, and even suicides. These may be very unsettling and cause you to want to move. Not everyone's perception will allow them to see residual energy as ghostly forms. These apparitions may appear very real but may have some unreal qualities that catch your attention. Often they will be dressed in period clothing and carry or be seen using tools from the past. They may carry out their routines as if nothing has happened to change them. A farmer may be milking a cow, a housewife may be doing laundry, a lovely young woman may be receiving a gentleman caller, and the list could go on and on. Many people have reported seeing ballroom dances and weddings in progress.

When houses are unknowingly built on the site of former battles, Indian burial grounds, or old cowboy encampments, bizarre events may be commonplace. This may add to the house's reservoir of energy, qualifying it as a genuine haunted house. If it's determined that the disturbance is a residual haunting, one should research the history of the inhabitants. Do historical research on the property and surrounding areas. Always look for a historical connection, unless of course there is something to indicate a more recent reason.

Other reports are more shocking and reportedly frightening as well. The homeowner or client may witness a murder or watch helplessly as a heinous crime is committed. Still others may watch in horror as a battle is waged between two opposing forces. There are many documented stories of Civil War soldiers still fighting long-past battles. An Internet search will provide one with access to additional information, as will books by Daniel Cohen and the articles "Civil War Ghosts" and "The Visions of Ghost Armies" from the files of *FATE* Magazine. These energies may be replayed as sounds and voices. Sounds of battle may be recorded due to the intensity of the emotional event. Cannons going off, shots being fired, screams, and orders being yelled to invisible soldiers may be heard.

When these scenes are witnessed, it is important to remember that the location is usually the reason for the disturbance. These scenes from the past become indelibly etched in the etheric atmosphere. Whenever someone undergoes a highly emotional or traumatic experience, it interpenetrates all surrounding vibrational frequencies; the essence of these events is then recorded. The more emotional the event, the longer it will last. The scenarios may last for centuries before the energy dissipates and disappears.

One lazy afternoon as I sat absorbed in reading an exciting account of the Civil War, my very psychic nine-year-old granddaughter approached me with an odd request. She said, "I think we should go ghost hunting." She had never been on a ghost hunt so this really surprised me. Being the super grandmother that I am, I decided right then and there that we could do a field investigation. There is a cemetery in our town that was created in the early 1800s, and for some time I had wanted to check it out for paranormal activity. I called my daughter, who was babysitting another grandchild, and asked her if they would like to explore the cemetery with us. She said she was bored and the adventure would be perfect to break up her routine. So off we went— my daughter, two grandchildren ages nine and seven, and me—loaded with cameras, dowsing rods, EMF detectors, and all the things the children (future ghost hunters) could use safely. It was about four o'clock in the afternoon and extremely hot, so I didn't anticipate staying any longer than it would take to satisfy my granddaughter's questing spirit.

Shortly after we arrived at the cemetery, the kids began taking pictures and making more noise than a gaggle of geese. If ghosts only appear when it is quiet, we were certainly out of luck. Well, as luck would have it, I was witness to an amazing paranormal event! Although it was exciting, it was also confusing and disappointing at the same time.

It was amazing because I saw an old automobile, possibly a Model T, as it entered the cemetery. It was confusing and disappointing because I did not have the presence of mind to take a picture of it and its occupants before it dissipated into thin air!

What happened was that the kids were standing near the edge of the paved roadway in the cemetery, preparing to cross. I turned to see a dark vehicle fast approaching. My first instinct, of course, was for the safety of the children. I quickly shoved them out of the way. They yelled a resounding "What's wrong, NanNa?" I thought they looked a little puzzled as I scolded them saying, "Couldn't you see that car?" They both looked so dumbfounded and for the life of me I could not figure out why. Then slowly I began to comprehend what had happened. They had not seen what I had seen! My next thought was that I had failed to capture it on film. There I stood, camera in hand, and not a clue as to what was happening!

The fact that I was instinctively protecting the children totally blocked my perception. I saw the antique car as a very solid object; it did not register as a ghostly phenomena but only as a potential threat to the children. Isn't it odd how our minds can alter the truth of our reality?

I can tell you that I noticed three people in the car; there was a woman who appeared to be dressed in Roaring Twenties attire, and there were possibly two men, but I am not sure about the driver. My daughter was fascinated by the entire event and wanted to stay longer, hoping the car would return and we could capture a photograph of it.

However, as with so many opportunities to photograph or record paranormal activities, there are no second chances. I believe the automobile and its occupants were all forms of residual ghosts. It's possible that they had all been killed in an automobile accident and that day was the anniversary of their deaths, or they may appear daily. I think we will be spending a lot of spare time researching as well as investigating in that particular cemetery. Maybe we will be lucky and get a second chance. Stranger things have happened!

As for the children, they photographed ecto-mist and a few daytime orbs so they were very excited. I treated them to dinner that night at their favorite restaurant because I really felt bad about scaring them in the cemetery. Although they had already forgotten it by nightfall, I am pretty sure they think their grandmother is an insane woman at times, but they love me anyway!

SIX

SHADOW GHOSTS

The Shadow: some hide, others reveal.

ANTONIO PORCHIA (1885–1968)

No matter how much time and energy we spend trying to understand paranormal phenomena, we sometimes come across ghostly manifestations that almost defy explanation, things that do not quite fit our preconceived ideas of how things should look, or actually be, for that matter.

"Shadow ghosts" have started showing up in photographs and are demanding our attention. These mysterious unknown entities are so named because of the dark images they leave on photographs. Although they are seldom seen visually, they are easily captured by the camera, and most of the time it is by accident. They often appear startled when caught unawares. This leads me to wonder if they are just passing through our dimension. Besides the dark mysterious images they conjure up, they also generate a lot of questions. Who are they and what are they? Are they demons? Are they evil? Obviously they are the representative energy of someone who has moved from our vibrational frequency (life) into a new invisible dimensional frequency. Energy is the essence of who we are in this lifetime. It survives the death of the physical body. When it is seen, heard, felt, or photographed by someone, it is because it has a purpose and wants to be acknowledged by us.

This shadowy energy form has been actively seen and photographed by unsuspecting people as well as ghost hunters and paranormal investigators. A sudden new interest in ghost hunting has made it acceptable to the general public to be more open to ghost hunting and paranormal phenomena. Perhaps this is why more and more images of shadow ghosts are being recognized and presented as paranormal phenomena.

When we think about shadows, it is usually in relation to our own shadow. However, every day many people catch fleeting glimpses of something out of their peripheral vision. Could this be the elusive shadow ghost rushing into an unseen dimension beyond ours? Have you ever noticed how shadows seem to creep stealthily in front of you, only to disappear instantly? Have you ever sat in your home and thought you saw a shadow across the room, beyond a doorway, or down the hall? Have you ever been awakened during the night to see a shadow in your room? If you have, you probably encountered a shadow ghost as it passed through our realm of existence.

Shadows have been part of our reality since childhood. Even Peter Pan's shadow took on a mystical quality as it danced across the movie screen. So it's really no wonder that we don't recognize shadow ghosts as such when we see them. Although we are basically unaware of their presence, they are able to come and go within our dimension. They share our space. Or do we share theirs?

Theories abound regarding shadow ghosts. Ghost hunters and researchers agree that they appear as dark human figures without any discernible features. They appear strangely similar in shape and form. The one noticeable difference is their height, which has been photographed to appear as short as two feet tall or up to five to seven feet tall in relation to their surroundings.

The very word *ghost* conjures up visions of eerie, misty shadows and wispy figures floating in the darkness. Add to this a dark, unfamiliar entity and you have all the makings of a Hollywood ghost movie! Exactly why ghosts appear as shadowy silhouettes is unknown, but when we substitute the word *vibration* or *frequency* for *ghost,* we come closer to understanding these bizarre manifestations of energy.

Discarnate souls have a very distinct personal vibration. Although this frequency varies according to the deceased's level of spiritual evolvement, a dark vibration does not necessarily mean an evil presence.

We normally see only a small section of the electromagnetic energy spectrum. The part visible to us indicates the colors we perceive: red, orange, yellow, green, blue, indigo, and violet. However, as light energy travels at different speeds and through different energy fields, the colors change. Because ghosts are electromagnetic energy, they have the ability to materialize in a multitude of colors, including black.

I don't believe that shadow ghosts are casting a shadow at all. I believe that ghosts are seen and photographed at different vibrational frequencies. This is due in part to a photographer's ability to resonate with the frequency of the ghost as they perceive their energy.

Commonly mistaken for demons due to their dark presence, shadow ghosts have been assigned an evil persona. There is no proof that they are any more evil than any other ghost or spirit. As a matter of fact, I have witnessed a huge mass of green ecto-mist while in a cemetery late at night that made me more apprehensive than any shadow ghost ever could. And no, ghosts cannot and will not follow you home! They generally stay connected to a particular location or person.

I believe it is the word *shadow* that adds to the confusion and misunderstanding of this ghostly form. We have been programmed since childhood to believe that black is evil or negative and white is good or positive. Remember how all the bad cowboys wore black hats and the good ones wore white hats? Black brings up images of darkness, evil, wickedness, and sinister beings that are often demonic in nature. For some people just thinking about "black" or "darkness" makes them anxious and nervous.

Are shadow ghosts evil? The answer is no! Our universe supplies us daily with positive light and energy. It is humans in their quest for power, control, and greed that create the evil in our realm of existence.

Remember, ghosts do not have the power to control you. You have more power than they do because of your physical body. Your energy is self-contained; you are an unlimited source of positive energy; you have an abundance of energy at your beck and call whether you acknowledge it or not; you have the power to ward off negative energy in whatever form it presents itself. Ghosts cannot make you do anything against your will.

So if you photograph or see a shadow ghost, accept it for what it is—an energized intelligent form that was just caught unawares as it passed through our realm of existence. Acknowledge its presence and wish it well on its journey.

SEVEN

IMAGINARY PLAYMATES

"The school is not quite deserted," said the Ghost. "A solitary child, neglected by his friends, is left there still!"

CHARLES DICKENS (1812–1870)

One of your first calls to investigate a ghost may be due to ghosts who are frightening children. Although children may be involved and ghosts will most certainly be there, you may be surprised to find that it's the parents who are frightened.

Let me begin by saying that children are the most resilient people on earth. They take everything in stride and this includes ghosts as well as paranormal phenomena. They see them, they hear them, and they usually don't question that they are real. They've not yet been programmed to believe that there is no such thing as a ghost.

Unfortunately, some parents unknowingly teach their children to ignore the possibility of ghosts. Although they may be doing it out of fear or misunderstanding, they are negating their children's reality. Most of the time, children are too young to be influenced by religion, society, government, or television and therefore relate to ghosts very easily. Children, for the most part, are open and receptive to ghosts. It's their parents who are fearful. They were probably programmed at an early age not to accept the reality of ghosts; after all, ghosts are not a scientifically proven fact.

During the investigative interview with the parents, encourage them to tell their story. But, if at all possible, interview the child a short distance away from the parents to see what is really going on. You may hear the child say things like "Oh, that's just so-and-so. He just wants to be my friend!" They might also say, "She or he used to live here and they like my toys." The responses could be very enlightening, and they could give you a clear indication of where to focus and where to place your equipment, recorders, and cameras.

If the child is truly frightened, an investigator may be in a position to help ease their fears by explaining the cause of the disturbance. When and if this happens, don't talk down to the child. They are far more capable of understanding ghosts than anyone may realize. In fact, they probably already know the answer and just need to be validated. Ghosts are attracted to children and will often stay nearby to protect them.

Such was the case for my grandson Michael, who was eight years old at the time of this incident. Late one night he ran from his bedroom into the living room where his parents were watching television. He appeared very frightened and kept repeating over and over, "There is a boy jumping on my bed!" His parents thought he was making it up so he could stay up late and watch television. They scolded him and sent him back to bed. Well, the next night was a replay of the first, with him appearing to be even more frightened. "Back to bed!" was his parents' answer to his dilemma. However, on the third night when a very frightened, tearful child declared that there was a ghost in his room who was jumping on his bed, his parents let him stay up late with them. A couple of hours later while he was sleeping soundly on the sofa in the living room, a drunk driver lost control of his car and slammed into Michael's bedroom exactly where his bed was! There is absolutely no doubt in our minds that his mysterious visitor saved Michael's life.

SIGNS OF GHOST CHILDREN

Hearing laughter in a house or building is a sure indication of ghost children at play. They may chatter away as they entertain each other. Giggles are often heard, and it's not unusual to hear these gleeful sounds, especially around the holidays. Crying or sobbing may be heard, as well as muffled, tearful sounds of sadness. Footsteps running back and forth are one of the most common signs of ghost children in the house. They may also make thumping sounds as they jump up and down on beds, furniture, and the floor. Often the sound of balls bouncing and toys making noises can be heard. Mechanical toys may start and stop on their own, creating a spooky atmosphere. Although this is usually not upsetting to children, it can be very unsettling for the parents.

Almost any sound a child would make can be duplicated by a ghost child. They may appear sad, angry, or happy depending upon the circumstances surrounding their deaths. Talking to them openly and sincerely may be all that is needed to stop the disturbance or allow them the freedom to leave. Ghost children, just like our children, are very perceptive and will pick up on a sham in an instant, which may have a negative effect on your investigation.

If an investigator is able to communicate with the ghost through the child or through ghost-hunting equipment, they may learn that the ghost wishes to stay. If this is the case, an explanation to the parents about setting up house rules and boundaries for the ghosts would be in order. This includes the children in the house too, so they will also understand everything that is going on.

A very common occurrence is children who have imaginary playmates. How much can be attributed to their imaginations and how much can be attributed to a ghost? I believe that almost all such childhood interaction is real communication with unseen visitors: family and friends from other realms.

My first Thanksgiving without my father was very memorable indeed. My granddaughter Brittany, who was three at the time, was at my house along with family and friends. I have a huge old oak desk and she loved to crawl underneath it and play. On this particular day she had slipped off to play with her cousins. I sent my husband to find her so she could be seated at the table. He came back up the hallway with the strangest look on his face. I said, "What is it? What is wrong?" "You had better come with me," he said.

I trailed after him and into the den where she was. There she sat under my desk, and she had the oddest look on her sweet little face. I knelt down and asked her, "Honey, what is wrong?" "Why didn't you tell me Papa Dick was dead?" she responded defiantly. I reeled back with surprise as the tears came streaming down my face. "How do you know this? Why are you saying this?" I asked her. "Because he has been talking to me and he told me! Why didn't you tell me?" Well, by this time I was at a loss for words and overcome with emotions. Here I was in the middle of a wonderful family gathering trying to process what had just happened with my precious little granddaughter. Of course it became the topic of conversation during our meal. And to add more to the story, my two five-year-old grandsons started laughing, obviously sharing their own private joke. When we asked them what was going on, they replied, "Well, that's nothing, Papa Dick has been playing with us all day!" Well, you guessed it, by now I was emotionally drained. Obviously my father was there, and the grandchildren had seen him, interacted with him, and talked to him. What a Thanksgiving day to be remembered and how spiritually empowering to know that he is still with us!

Before one can talk to a ghost, it would be helpful to understand how they communicate. Children seem to have an innate knowledge of this process and have no fear of visiting with ghosts. The two most prominent forms of communication are verbal and telepathic. It would take an awesome presence to project a voice that could be heard audibly, and it would also take a tremendous amount of energy. However, it does happen and is not completely unheard of. I believe that much of what is perceived as audible by children is telepathic communication, although they do not understand how it happens.

My granddaughter Cheyenne, who was six going on twenty-six at the time, had a very real ghost playmate and still does to this day. I heard her one day chattering away as if she was having a wonderful conversation with someone so I slipped into the living room to see what she was up to. There she sat at the coffee table with a deck of cards in her hand. She was dealing them out and having a conversation with the empty space across from her. I said, "What are you doing?" She just laughed and replied, "I'm playing cards with Gabriella! Can't you see her?" She immediately returned to her one-sided conversation and continued to lay the cards on the table. I was beginning to think that she was putting me on, until I saw three cards move across the table to the other side, seemingly on their own accord! Okay, so now what? I just left her there playing with her friend until she became bored and moved on to other solitary pursuits, which she did shortly thereafter.

There have been so many instances of children talking and playing with invisible playmates that they simply cannot be discounted. Children have always had a special relationship with ghosts. It is not because they are more psychic or special in any way; they simply accept their reality as it actually is.

Adults everywhere believe in ghosts; they hear them, see them, and know that they are real, but they are reluctant to share their feelings for fear of ridicule. This fear blocks their perception of reality and will eventually create disharmony in their lives.

EIGHT

POLTERGEISTS

One need not be a chamber to be haunted;
One need not be a house;
The brain has corridors surpassing
Material place.

EMILY DICKINSON (1830–1886)

First and foremost, a poltergeist is *not* a ghost in any form of manifestation. Defining a poltergeist is a complex undertaking and to differentiate between a ghost and poltergeist activity is difficult as well. They both possess certain attributes of energy and display peculiar characteristics that compare to each other. This makes it even harder to understand what is really going on.

The word *poltergeist* is a German derivative that means "noisy ghost." This definition created the assumption that poltergeist activity was a ghostly manifestation of the most bizarre type. However, today a much better definition is recurrent spontaneous psychokinesis (RSPK). Poltergeists are, without a doubt, one of the most mysterious and most confusing elements of paranormal research. Although controversial in nature, they have been well documented and their existence is unquestionable.

As a ghost hunter or paranormal investigator, it is important to understand what is, and is not, a ghost. A poltergeist is not a ghost, a person, or an entity as such. It is an event. It is undirected energy, an emotional turbulence exhibited as a force to be dealt with. Literally!

As a rule, these events appear to be connected to a young person approaching the age of puberty. However, this is not always the case; the event could be generated from anyone, at any age, experiencing a personal crisis. I have witnessed poltergeist activity in my daughter who was twenty-two years old at the time and also in an elderly woman who was eighty-six years old. Obviously, it crosses the age barrier, and there are no boundaries as to race or sex.

Poltergeist activity appears when conflicts arise and cannot be resolved. These conflicts may be of a spiritual, emotional, physical, or even psychic nature. Typically, the person who generates the activity feels that they have no way to deal with the stress they are undergoing.

In my daughter's case, she was going through a traumatic divorce, and it affected her emotionally as well as spiritually. She came to stay with us, and, almost immediately upon her arrival, the activity began. The first night, books began to fly off the bookshelves and hit the floor with resounding force. Appliances began to act up, lights flickered on and off. What was normal rapidly became paranormal, literally overnight. After about two weeks we found ourselves living in a chaotic environment, never knowing what was going to happen next. Finally, out of sheer desperation, we demanded that she take control of her life, make some very hard decisions, and regain her power. The absolute minute she made these mental changes, it stopped! Although I was relieved, I was intrigued beyond belief. Never in my life had I witnessed something like that and, to be honest, I hope I never do again.

My second encounter happened during an investigation. Although I cannot relate the details due to client privilege, I can assure you that it was also an eerie event. One of the hardest things for me was to see the all-encompassing fear this event caused. I am not sure that this gentle person will ever recover. I can say that this particular poltergeist activity was due in part to a death: an overwhelming loss that may never be reconciled. During circumstances such as these, the best a ghost hunter or paranormal investigator can do is to educate the people involved. Fear is the absence of knowledge and when a person knows they are not alone and someone cares about them, things can change dramatically.

Poltergeist activity is an awesome force generated in the subconscious mind and is a direct result of repressed emotions that conceal resentment, frustration, repressed anger, or guilt; it could also be the result of the sexual stresses associated with puberty.

When families are suddenly exposed to this eerie, unexplainable phenomenon, their first reaction is fear. They may want to, or be directed to, call in someone to exorcise the house or, heaven forbid, the person involved. Exorcism is not effective and can make matters much worse, in my opinion.

The person involved, usually referred to as the "agent," may be in a rage, full of unresolved anger and resentment. They may feel powerless and may react much as a wounded animal would if approached aggressively. It would be appropriate to attempt to understand the source of the activity and focus on resolving the issues that have influenced it. Granted, a person or an entire family may feel as if they are being terrorized by the events as they unfold; however, information and knowledge of the activity will help them resolve their fears. Poltergeist activity is a very real event that produces very real effects. These effects are produced primarily by a person's inability to understand and control their inner power, their own unique energy.

If you feel uncomfortable confronting this issue, please refer the home owner or the client to a reputable parapsychologist for help in understanding this phenomenon.

More information regarding poltergeists may be obtained by reading *Poltergeists: Examining Mysteries of the Paranormal* by Michael Clarkson and also *Poltergeist! A Study in Destructive Haunting* by Colin Wilson. Poltergeist energy creates a wide range of activities. One of the most commonly mentioned is the mysterious pebbles and rocks that are tossed around. It has probably been one of the most reported events throughout history because of its destructive nature. Pebbles and stones may fly through the air with incredible speed, turning into dangerous projectiles. The stones can even be extremely hot or cold upon inspection. This just adds more intrigue to the phenomena.

Another well-documented effect is that of flying pots and pans, which relates to the phenomenon of a "kitchen ghost." Dishes may be broken and every conceivable kitchen utensil (including knives) may be thrown, tossed, or otherwise scattered about.

Throughout recorded history, rappings and loud powerful knocks have been heard. They range from light taps to loud bangs. If these are heard during the night or while alone in the house, they are almost always attributed to a ghost.

Small, bizarre fires with no discernible origin are frequently encountered and have been well documented. They are an intriguing effect of poltergeist activity and are potentially threatening as well. Small fires may spring up, be put out, and then resurface in another area of the house or in another structure on the property. Several fires may start at the same time, creating even more fear and confusion. As they blaze out of control with no apparent cause, they could easily destroy property and belongings. This particular aspect of poltergeist activity is very dangerous for everyone involved.

There are many effects of poltergeist activity. Other than flying rocks and fires, other phenomena include strange noises or objects that move about, furniture and household items that levitate, electrical appliances malfunctioning, and spectacular light displays. Another unusual event is that of accumulated water from unknown sources. It may appear as water sprinkling from overhead or mysterious water puddles on the floor. This event is very disconcerting to everyone involved.

I want to mention some rare events that, although they are poltergeist activity, may have a two-fold manifestation. These rare effects may manifest as actual visual apparitions. These manifestations and materializations of energy are bizarre and, when added to the complex nature of the "agent," can cause extreme distress to the agent and the family as well. Displaced energy is a mysterious force that can manifest anywhere and in any form. This energy can also be projected in many different ways.

I believe that when poltergeist events are reported and they contain the elements of voices being heard and apparitions being seen, there is much more going on than the traditional poltergeist activity. We know that ghosts can use and manipulate energy to their best advantage. Can you imagine their delight when coming into contact with someone who is generating enormous amounts of energy? Someone who is unconsciously projecting their energy all over the place without actual intent or regard to direction? What self-respecting ghost wouldn't take advantage of that situation? This would create a two-fold problem that would have to be dealt with as two distinct activities. One would be the manifestation of a ghost. Two would be of a psychological nature and would require in-depth counseling to alleviate the fear or anger often associated with poltergeist activity.

I also believe that when a child, adolescent, or adult has the power and energy to create these events, they are also very gifted. They have special psychic gifts of clairvoyance, healing, and clairaudience, as well as other gifts that will one day manifest as service to humanity. Their fullest potential may be realized as a counselor, healer, medium, or in other fields that represent spiritual, emotional, or physical growth.

As a matter of fact, part of the fear and frustration they feel may stem from not understanding their paranormal abilities. I would highly recommend to anyone who is investigating what they believe to be poltergeist activity to consult a credible psychic for added insight and information. Astrology and numerology will also give valuable clues about the personality involved as well as the psychic gifts they possess.

Poltergeist activity may appear as harmless, unusual manifestations around the house, and I suspect a lot more people experience this than they realize. This activity can also appear as humorous antics, as if someone had a practical joker living in their home.

When poltergeist activity begins, when these paranormal psychic forces are released, contacting a ghost hunter or paranormal investigator who is experienced in this field is the first step to resolving the issue. Remember: poltergeist activity is *not* a ghost. It is undirected, displaced energy in its most intense form.

NINE

GHOSTLY ORBS

Our departed braves, fond mothers,
glad, happy hearted maidens and even little children
who have lived here and rejoiced here for a brief season,
will love these somber solitudes and at eventide,
they shall greet shadowy returning spirits.

CHIEF SEATTLE, ORATION TREATY (1854)

My first experience with orb phenomena came at the age of twelve. I was sitting outside late one afternoon, deep in thought about an upcoming school event. Suddenly, from seemingly out of nowhere, a huge orange sphere appeared before me. It was a little above my direct sight and as large as a big beach ball. It was pulsating and its very distinct color would fade and deepen in intensity as I watched it. Very soon after I became aware of its presence, it began to move slowly toward me. I was stunned and sat very still thinking it would disappear if I failed to acknowledge it. Oh well, so much for wishful thinking. I was astonished as it gently floated right through my midsection! I gasped as I felt it pass through my body. I recall feeling giddy, and I was jittery for some time afterward.

My father arrived home from work, and I just couldn't wait to tell him about my experience. He gave me one of his ever-present "What-have-you-been-up-to-now?" looks as he scratched his head. I told him what had happened. His first expression was puzzlement as he pondered what to say. "Ball lightning," he said. "That's what it was. That's all it was—just ball lightning!" and with that he strolled out of the room.

If I was mystified before, I was really confused now. What the heck was ball lightning? His answer did nothing to calm my anxiety about it returning, to say nothing of stilling my inquisitive mind. Deep down I knew that I had experienced a spiritual visitation of some sort. I seemed to know that it was really *someone* and not *something* that had tried to communicate with me. Ball lightning, indeed!

After that first encounter with spherical energy, orbs began to show up in my photographs. It seemed that there was never a photograph of a family gathering, holiday, or school event without an orb or two in it. This began when I was using a very simple camera. I progressed to a Polaroid, which was followed by a 35-mm and eventually my ever-present Kodak digital camera. I have always had energy show up in orb form on my photos, and I definitely do not believe the theory that orbs are a product of a digital camera's inaccuracies. I am not going to even address orbs as dust, moisture, or insects. My experience, coupled with my clairvoyant awareness, renders this a waste of time as well as an insult to human intelligence. Furthermore, it's unlikely that any legitimate researcher would conduct an outside investigation in any form of precipitation. And regarding dust, I have been on a dirt road taking photographs of orb activity when a truck came by. This was the opportune time for me to test the dust theory, as I had just been able to photograph orbs in the stillness of evening with no one present. However, after the truck sped by, I was unable to photograph any orbs, even after the dust had settled. No dust spots showed up on my camera screen. Imagine that!

Now, what do I believe? In the search for a clear and concise definition of these mysterious orbs, it is easy to become confused by all the questions, definitions, vague answers, and skeptical responses—none of which can be proven scientifically—leaving us to form our own opinions concerning what is acceptable to our concept of reality. The rest must be stored for future reference and possible reevaluation. Our thoughts are energized frequencies, and by merely researching the field of orb activity, we can raise our spiritual vibrations and emerge farther along our spiritual pathway. Obviously any assessment of orbs would begin with a questing spirit. Hopefully this chapter will answer some of your questions and will encourage you to look beyond our realms of existence into new dimensions, albeit through the eye of the camera.

The first and foremost question is: Are orbs intelligent life-forms, and, if so, can they communicate with us? Next, one has to wonder: have the earth's vibrations changed or has something in nature been altered to allow us to see them more easily now? Are they simply observers in our dimension, or are they here to impart knowledge? Do their colors mean anything? And last but not least: are they ghosts? The questions are as unique and varied as the people who ask them. So let's begin with the most obvious observation: the shape.

I believe that spirit, which is pure energy, creates a spherical structure (compressed energy form) as a means of travel from one dimension to the next or through varying degrees of vibrational frequencies. According to the laws of physics, transformative energy (such as departed souls) would assume the natural shape of a sphere. This spherical shape encapsulates the essence of a spirit, manifesting as circular anomalies.

Ghosts and spirits can and do appear as orbs. Although elusive and mysterious, they do manifest for and resonate at the same frequency as the person or persons photographing them. Orbs in photos may not be very impressive, but to see them on video is very exciting indeed! I have seen them move at rapid speeds, darting back and forth while interacting with the camera. I have witnessed them grow larger while performing antics such as moving in a spiral, floating upwards and downwards as well as sideways. I have also seen them respond to questions and respond positively to requests to appear. I have seen them hiding behind objects as if playing hide-and-seek. And seek them we do.

By taking a closer look at orbs as compressed electromagnetic spiritual energies, we can separate orb phenomena into three distinct groups: ghost orbs, spirit orbs, and oracle orbs.

GHOST ORBS

Before any definition can be put forth, it must be noted that we only see what we believe exists as part of our reality. Discarnate energies retain their emotions, personalities, and intelligence. Their life force (soul) extends beyond death and is capable of manifesting as a ghost orb. Orbs require less energy than full-bodied ghosts, enabling them to exist more easily in our dimensional frequency. At times they are able to appear denser or larger and they can manifest as a partial or full apparition.

Ghost orbs display an inner substance, and, very often in photographs, a nucleus is visible. They also present a thicker outer layer or ring. They may also display an electromagnetic glow around them. Sometimes they appear less spherical in shape given their density and composition and appear a little lopsided. We have a photograph of one that looks like a giant black-eyed pea.

Ghost orbs have been photographed during the day as well as at night. They are usually very active and seldom stationary for very long. Seemingly always on the move, they will appear in one picture and then disappear in the next. They also tend to follow people around and can be captured on camera by simply turning around rapidly or snapping your camera over your shoulder. They are attracted to people and frequent the same places as the living; in fact anywhere and everywhere there are people, ghost orbs can be found.

Most ghost orbs can be categorized in three distinct energy forms. Transparent, which is crystal clear and easy to see through; translucent, which is semi-transparent and therefore harder to see through; and opaque ghost orbs which are the thickest and show the greatest depth. They are so solid they can cast shadows. This is viewed as excellent evidence of ghosts. They can also emit their own energy impulses as light and often appear very bright in photographs. To make themselves visible to us, they lower their vibrations to the point of transparency, and then they continue to lower their vibrations until they are very dense, which leads to full visibility as ecto-mist or possibly a full-bodied ghostly apparition.

Ghost orbs are able to move at very rapid speeds. They change directions at will, appear and disappear, and even seem to be hiding in some photographs. They are curious by nature and actively seek out unsuspecting visitors.

Ghost orbs are photographed almost everywhere there is a reported haunting. They have been photographed at the scenes of tragic accidents or at sites where tragedies occurred. Battlefields, cemeteries, and abandoned buildings are also very active sites for ghost orbs.

For the most part, ghost orbs simply want to attract attention. Perhaps they want to be noticed in order to convey a message to someone who is receptive to them. They may have some unfinished business that they are about. Remember, we cannot see them unless they want us to.

SPIRIT ORBS

Everything that exists does so due to vibrations. The universe as we know and understand it is an expression of visible and invisible pulsations of light energy. When this light energy emerges from another dimension, it slows down and the resulting frequencies determine how that light energy appears. This affects the color of every energy form we see, including orbs.

These unique electromagnetic orbs are known as spirit orbs. These orbs are discarnate souls that have transformed to lighter, higher frequencies, not feeling the need or desire to continue to manifest in our realm of existence. They do, however, come back and forth to check on people to whom they are connected.

Spirit orbs are loved ones who have passed over. Family, friends, and even spirit guides can and do appear in this form. If you have seen or photographed a colorful orb in your home or on your property, it very well could be a loved one who dropped in to say hello. If you will ask telepathically to be shown who it is, you will immediately get a sense of the person who has paid you a visit.

Spirit orbs manifest in many colors and varying sizes. Some are extremely large and others are very small. Their size is determined by how much energy they emit, while their colors are determined by the vibration of their unique electromagnetic fields.

We perceive different colors because we are exposed to varying wavelengths of light. Spirit orbs vibrate at unique frequencies that create color wavelengths invisible to the human eye, but they can be captured with the camera's eye. Each spirit orb has its own personal vibration and level of evolvement.

Soft, white spirit orbs are younger souls who have recently entered new dimensional frequencies. They are often small and emit pale hues. Pale pinks, blues, greens, and yellows fall into this category. More evolved souls appear deeper in color. Red, dark pink, blue, green, amber, indigo, and magenta represent these luminous soul bearers.

Older, more advanced souls appear in rainbow colors. They are amazing to capture in photographs and are representative of a commanding spiritual presence.

Spirit orbs are here to help us on our spiritual quest by offering comfort, validation, and even assistance in our times of need.

They seem to exhibit personalities and respond to telepathy; they are very telepathic by nature and welcome communication in this way. I have seen them twinkle when a telepathic message was acknowledged! They interact with people on a personal, emotional level and are capable of expressing feelings. That's why they are often photographed hovering over or near one specific person. They want to be acknowledged in order to effectively render assistance when needed. They are nurturing and caring, and their desire is to advance us farther along our spiritual pathways.

An interesting investigation took place on private land that had a secluded wooded area filled with anomalies and huge orb clusters. Katie, a good friend and fellow ghost hunter, and I went along with my husband to see if the area was active. We were hoping for activity and we were not disappointed. Katie and I sat on the tailgate of the truck as my husband drove us around in total darkness. We were able to document several different anomalies, including orbs of every size and color imaginable. There were large ones and small ones, some with great depth and texture, and some very vibrant ones as well. One orb in particular seemed to take a special interest in Katie. As she was watching it on the screen of her digital night-shot camera, it began to move forward. She began to interact with it by asking it to grow larger on the count of three. We nearly fell off the tailgate of the truck as it grew large enough to fill her entire screen, and then it shrank back to its smaller size. Again she asked it to grow larger on the count of three, or "puff up" as she put it, and again it expanded to fill the screen. Excitedly, she asked it once again to enlarge, which it did on the count of three. This time it changed its color from yellow to a much brighter golden hue. Wow, what an intelligent interaction. Suddenly, her batteries went dead! Not having other batteries handy, she lost contact with her spirit orb. (Here is a good reason to always have extra batteries on hand.) Of course who's to say that they could not have been drained? We do know that ghosts can use batteries as an energy source to "recharge" themselves.

ORACLE ORBS

Oracle orbs are the seers of the universe and, as such, they are very prophetic by nature. They are highly intelligent and their goal is to impart inspirational knowledge and wisdom. They are in a receptive state waiting to be reincarnated into physical form. Given this information, it is very important to take notice of where they are seen or photographed. They have a very specific reason for being there. They resonate to your own very unique vibrational frequency and have allowed you to see them for an important reason. If you have photographed an oracle orb, you have been given a very special gift.

If you look closely enough, you may see facial features, a face, or even an entire bodily form inside the orb. If so, you have captured an oracle orb. You may recognize this discarnate soul as a relative, an ancestor, or someone dear to you who has transformed to another dimension. The message is clear: "I am returning soon!" Remember it is not a coincidence that you were able to photograph them; you were gifted with spiritual knowledge in the form of an orb.

If the face appears as someone unfamiliar to you—perhaps a monk, a soldier, an angel, or simply someone you have never seen before—you are being asked to accept a message. Be receptive to whatever form this message takes because it will be meant for you. Sometimes, animals will appear in oracle orbs. They may be discarnate pets or one's own personal totem animal, which is a message in itself.

Oracle orbs are the essence of the soul. They can easily take their former shape at will, becoming full-bodied manifestations of energy if desired. When and if this happens there will be no room for debate as to what you have witnessed.

Oracle orbs are able to transcend matter, pass through portals such as doors and mirrors, and even pass through your physical body. If they do float through you, they have chosen to blend their unique energy with yours for a specific reason known only to you. Never doubt this! Also never fear this. It is a gift, and they mean you no harm.

They are capable of clairaudient transmissions, emitting a voice that you can easily hear. It is only our perception of them that blocks active communication. In addition to sending their telepathic messages, when we remain open and unblocked, they can easily share whatever messages they may have for us.

Oracle orbs are often photographed visiting the home of expectant parents before a birth, signaling the return of an encapsulated soul into a new incarnation. They visit loved ones who are preparing for the transformation of death. They are also present at times when a life crisis looms on the horizon and during times of extreme chaos. They appear in photographs at weddings, funerals, family reunions, almost anywhere they are needed. They are soul contacts, soul mates, and as avatars they are imbued with special attributes. These special qualities enable them to carry out their missions. If you have photographed an oracle orb, treasure your picture, for you have most certainly received a spiritual message.

On the same property where we captured our interactive spirit orb, I also photographed an extremely large oracle orb. There appears within the orb a man who is kneeling down or, as some have suggested, sitting on a horse. He is surrounded by spirit orbs: radiant pink, robin's egg blue, and green, as well as many that are less colorful but just as plentiful.

Orbs, in all their varying degrees of energy, offer us a new perspective on spirituality, encouraging us to open our senses to new dimensions of reality and prepare for global shifts of vibrational frequencies.

Capturing orbs on film during an investigation is extremely important, even though they are becoming rather commonplace. Never discount their spiritual value when reviewing and assessing your photographs. They can point you to interesting areas of activity as well as unexplored depths of your own spirituality.

TEN

ECTO-MIST

Do I believe in ghosts? No, but I am afraid of them.

MARIE ANNE DU DEFFAND (1697–1780)

"Ectoplasm" was a well-known term used at the turn of the century. It was used originally to describe a mysterious opaque substance that materialized from spirit mediums during a séance. More recently, the words ectoplasm or "ecto-mist" are now associated with ghost hunting and paranormal research. They are used to describe the vaporous mists that show up in ghost-hunting photographs. Now believed to be the second stage of ghostly manifestation (orbs being the first), these ethereal mists have been photographed in many places all over the world.

As with any unexplained phenomena, there are always the skeptics who, either out of ignorance or fear of the unknown, step forward to debunk these unique paranormal phenomena. When it shows up in photographs, there are skeptics who dismiss it as smoke, fog, the photographer's breath, moisture, or even automobile exhaust. These all fall prey to skeptical analysis. But since most ecto-mist is not seen by the photographer's naked eye at the time the picture was taken, we must rely on the credibility and integrity of the photographer. First of all, any serious researcher or investigator will take every precaution to prevent natural occurrences from being in the area. A serious researcher would never smoke or exhale in cold weather while taking pictures during an investigation. They would also refrain from taking pictures in the rain or around campfires and bonfires, in fact anywhere smoke could travel or form swirling mists.

Ecto-mist is a ghost at a particular stage of manifestation. As the condensed energy in orb form is released, it begins to swirl, spread, and separate. Ghosts, as well as spirits, begin to appear as smoky semitranslucent mists. These ethereal mists of ectoplasm do not normally show a recognizable shape due to the lack of electromagnetic energy needed for full materialization.

In order for ectoplasm to materialize into a full-bodied ghost or apparition there needs to be an adequate energy supply. Ghosts pull this energy from many sources such as batteries, power lines, electrical outlets, and appliances, as well as the human electrical system. That's us!

Ecto-mist has been photographed in many colors with varying degrees of white and gray as the most prominent. However, many peculiar mists have been caught on film in extraordinary colors of red, green, blue, indigo, and black.

Ecto-mist may appear as a thick fog or as a wispy, fine mist floating effortlessly in the wind. These mists are always around us at some stage of materialization. We are unable to see them because of the difference in our vibrational frequencies.

Our very essence is a frequency vibration, so it stands to reason that ghosts who have survived death can and do resonate to us as they manifest their own unique energies. Although ecto-mist is a uniquely mysterious phenomenon, it does have consciousness as well as a desire to communicate.

Energy in the form of ecto-mist is capable of expressing extraordinary shapes. The vibrational rate creates and enhances the density of ecto-mist. These foggy mists will often display unique body parts as attempts at materialization are made. Mist may appear with arms, hands, legs, or partial bodies, either seen inside the mist or sticking out of it.

When photographs containing ecto-mist are magnified, they often display well-defined facial features. Perhaps it is possible for spirit to manifest faces within the mist as a form of communication. Ecto-mist can appear anywhere at any time.

Recently I went with my husband to check on some cattle. While he was busy with the calves, I strolled over to a wooded area to take some pictures. My camera is never far from my side, and as a result I have an album full of fantastic ghost pictures. On this particular day at about six in the evening, I asked to be shown something that I had never seen before. I also asked for something that I could recognize as appearing specifically for me to validate the existence of ghosts. Getting orbs in my photographs has become rather commonplace so what I really wanted was a different anomaly. Well, what I got was certainly more than I had requested! Not really expecting anything, I didn't bother to check the camera until I got home and put the pictures on my computer. That was when I saw it! First it looked like a swirling, light-blue mist near two rolls of hay. I enlarged it once, and I thought I could see faint facial features. Okay, to be truthful, I wondered if I was imagining it. However, a second magnification revealed the well-defined face of a Victorian woman. She looked very much like a delicate cameo. Guess what? I collect cameos! Was this materialization just for me? I believe it was! Will I return to this site for further investigation? My husband has jokingly told everyone that wild horses couldn't keep me away, and boy, is he right! I may not help feed the cows, but I will definitely be taking a lot of pictures out there.

What really excites me is that we just never know when a ghost will appear. They are ever-present and seeking to communicate their existence to us to let us know that there is no death and we do not die; we are merely transformed.

Ecto-mist has been photographed everywhere. Generally it is photographed outside in cemeteries or at sites where battles were fought, at historical places, as well as in and around abandoned buildings. Think about the sites where ecto-mist appears. Hundreds of years ago they probably looked very different. Buildings are torn down and replaced. In fact, entire towns have disappeared only to be replaced by new structures, but the land remains. To a ghost who is trapped in time, the previous structures appear the same as they once were. It doesn't matter how they appear today; their sense of it remains in the past. Just as I was able to photograph a Victorian woman on the edge of a hay meadow, you can also capture ecto-mist in many unlikely places. Remember: cemeteries are not the only places where ghosts dwell.

Ecto-mist usually appears at sites where numerous orbs are found. These orbs are floating about gathering energy, possibly for transformation into ecto-mist and even full-bodied manifestations of a ghost or apparition.

Unlike orbs that seem to dart in and out of our realm of existence playing their game of "now you see me, now you don't" or "catch me if you can," ecto-mist seems to linger and grow and move about as if watching us and what we are doing. Its presence at cemeteries is eerie, to say the least. Many ghost hunters have gasped to see pictures of each other with ecto-mist appearing right next to them, as well as some mist which seems to cover them totally!

Late one night at a local cemetery, a huge green mist appeared to be following one of our investigators. The photograph shows very obvious movement as well as a rather menacing approach. To be honest, our field investigator, who was on his first ghost hunt, was pretty shaken and not too sure whether or not he wanted to go on another.

Photographing unseen energies is a process that never becomes boring. Now that cameras are more sensitive to deeper spectrums of light frequencies, we are able to see ghostly mists and exciting phenomena that were previously hidden from us.

ELEVEN

VORTEX: A GHOSTLY CONVEYANCE

The road goes on and on,
Down from the door where it began.
Now far ahead the road has gone,
And I must follow, if I can,
Pursuing it with eager feet,
Until it joins some larger way
Where many paths and errands meet,
And whither then? I cannot say.

J. R. R. TOLKIEN (1892–1973)

A vortex is probably the least understood of all ghostly phenomena. It almost defies definition, especially when outspoken skeptics are so quick to shout, "Camera strap!"

Although I may be standing on shaky ground in my attempt to explain vortexes, I do have my own personal experiences and photographs to add validity to my definition. If a picture is worth a thousand words, the subject of vortexes is certainly a place where photographic evidence is needed. Amid theory and speculation, little seems to be known about this controversial subject. Ghost-hunting websites such as www.ghoststudy.com often show examples of vortexes in their various stages of manifestation and is a good place for beginners to search for unusal paranormal anomalies.

I suppose if one is to arrive at a plausible explanation for vortexes, they must first address the issue of the camera strap no matter how unnecessary it seems. Skeptics would have us believe that because a majority of vortexes appear right of center in a photograph that it is a camera strap. I have purposefully tried to take a picture with the camera strap in the photo, and it is not as easy as it is proposed to be. Just because the vortex appears on the right-hand side does not mean that it is a strap. Many anomalous forms have been photographed with vortexes on the left-hand side as well as in the middle. They have also been pictured in various positions in the photograph. Unless it is blatantly obvious that it is a camera strap, don't be too quick to judge a photograph unworthy as paranormal evidence. With time and experienced eyes, combined with other collaborating factors, it will be easy to determine the presence of a vortex.

Now that we know what a vortex is not, let's explore what it could be and probably is.

WHAT DOES A VORTEX LOOK LIKE?

Most vortexes are unseen by the photographer, only showing up as movement of a supernatural energy form after the picture has been taken. Vortexes appear in a tubular shape and are often referred to as a funnel ghost. It has been suggested that they are whirling currents of energy that contain many orbs. Both of these definitions have merit and possibilities, as we will see.

Vortexes have been photographed as long, thick, fibrous, ropelike phenomena with an opaque appearance. Similarly, they've been pictured as dense white columns with protruding orbs. They may also appear to have a distinct rippled effect on the outer edges. Colors may vary with the frequency of the vibrations, from bright white to bluish white; pale hues of pink, gray, and lavender have been photographed. Extraordinary and unusual black vortexes have also been captured on film.

Vortexes are almost always photographed in a vertical position. However, some are seen swaying in unique horizontal positions. They may appear in front of people and objects as well as behind them. They have been photographed overhead and beneath things. They have been pictured casting shadows and appear to be alive with energy. Many photographs show vortexes in pairs, and they may even appear as multiple columns in the same instance.

SWIRL OF SOULS

Why do vortexes exist? What is their purpose? Intriguing questions!

I believe that a vortex represents a conduit that supplies the energy necessary for ghosts to retain their spherical shape until they choose to manifest in a more distinct form. To clarify this analysis, it is helpful to note that a vortex in its spiraling fluid movement is basically frictionless. To maintain a vortex structure, a continuous energy supply is needed. The vibrational spinning movement creates a permanent flow of energy. This energy is essentially a broad spectrum of vibrational frequencies that allows a ghost to draw from a constant energy source.

Ghosts find this very conducive to their ethereal existence. They create and encapsulate themselves inside a swirling vortex, using it as a frequency conveyance that allows them to retain their energized essence without losing their collective energy. In this way, they remain in a constant vibrational state until they decide to manifest on a larger scale, such as ecto-mist or a full-bodied apparition. Traveling in a vortex provides ghosts with the pathway of least resistance. This allows them to travel inter-dimensionally in a swirling or spinning motion and often at very rapid speeds.

The direction of the spiral vortex indicates the movement of energy. Vortexes that appear to swirl in a counterclockwise motion are descending in movement. Vortexes that spin in a clockwise motion will appear as rising. When spinning in clockwise motion, vortexes usually appear as straight, vertical, cylindrical forms with their density dependent upon the concentration of orbs inside. Often these orbs will be seen as protruding and in the process of exiting the vortex to float freely in our realm of existence.

However, when a vortex is in a counterclockwise spiral, it is often photographed as descending from the upper part of a photo. These descending vortexes are usually photographed as long swaying shapes swinging horizontally across the picture. They may appear to be bending and curving in motion with odd contrails behind them.

A vortex's inherent power lies in the concentration of ghost orbs it contains. As the orbs gather energy, the vortex itself becomes denser, and the rapid spinning vibration gives the illusion of solid matter. As with ghosts, many sources contribute to the vortex's energy base, such as electrical outlets, appliances, power stations, batteries, and the human energy system. All of these can be accessed by ghosts to enhance their energy supplies or to meet their manifestation needs.

As the orbs begin to exit the vortex and manifest as ecto-mist or a ghostly form, sudden electrical surges are created in the electromagnetic field surrounding the vortex. These are easily picked up with an EMF detector and can be sensed and felt by ghost hunters as well. As the orbs inside the vortex shift frequencies, they are propelled outward and are often photographed during this process.

Vortexes are often photographed in homes during family gatherings. Perhaps this is due to the fact that soul groups choose to travel in a vortex to pay a visit to family and friends. Indeed, many photographs that contain vortexes are taken during holidays, at birthday parties, family reunions, and, last but not least, in cemeteries.

Vortexes are found outside as well as inside. They are found in churches, cemeteries, old structures, theaters, hotels, abandoned buildings, on battlefields—in fact, anywhere and everywhere they choose.

Vortexes are most often photographed where there is a lot of paranormal activity. I do not believe, however, that they are stationary. I feel they are in a constant state of movement even when found at one specific site for a period of time. As they swirl and spin, they carry their spiritual guests to their desired destinations, hopefully to be photographed by avid ghost researchers.

Vortexes are not as rare as they may seem, so they can be well worth the time and energy spent in their pursuit.

TWELVE

PORTALS FOR
INTER-DIMENSIONAL TRAVEL

The world is so empty if one thinks only
of mountains, rivers, and cities,
But to know someone here and there
who thinks and feels with us,
And though distant, is close to us in Spirit,
This makes the earth for us an inhabited garden.

JOHANN VON GOETHE (1749–1832)

Recently, a spontaneous field trip yielded a ghost hunter's "pot of gold." It was late afternoon when a friend called to tell me that she had just located the exact site of a reportedly haunted bridge. We had been trying to find it for months, and she hadn't given up until she had found it. Actually the place name is "Cry-Baby-Creek."

As the story goes, a young mother was driving across the bridge during the winter months, lost control of her car, and careened into the icy waters of the creek below. Both mother and baby drowned, and supposedly one who parks on the bridge late at night can hear the baby crying.

My ghost-hunting enthusiasm surfaced, and I agreed to meet my friend along with several other people to go out and see what we could find. It was about eight PM when we arrived; it was extremely hot, another reason I was a little dubious about venturing out. There was no sign of a breeze stirring and I knew the mosquitoes would be bad, not to mention the bats we encountered.

However, my good-natured friends soon lifted my somber mood, and we began a serious inquiry into the site. The two bridges were about two hundred feet apart. Now we had a dilemma. Which bridge was it? We parked our cars between the two bridges and tried to decide which one was the haunted bridge. The friend who had shown us the location had mentioned that earlier in the week she had become queasy while standing on the first bridge. With this in mind, we decided to focus on that bridge first.

Throughout the evening, we all made the trek back to the other bridge to test for activity. Several of those present were sensitive to unfamiliar energies as well as psychic. Everyone was in complete agreement: they felt nothing, heard nothing, nor did they sense anything. However, while at the first bridge, many expressed feelings of sadness, nervousness, and anxiety. We easily determined which side of the bridge the accident occurred on. Numerous orbs began to appear on our digital camera screens, and it was obvious that the activity was picking up.

As I watched my screen, I noticed something odd. There were clusters of something brown hanging on the branches of the trees overlapping the creek. Closer observation revealed bats! I have to tell you, I was ready to go right then and there. However, I intuitively felt that I should stay just a little longer to see if anything happened.

Then I heard it! A whisper-soft whirring sound as if there was a fan running off in the distance somewhere. We were deep in a wooded area on a country road with no lights or power sources nearby, so where was the sound coming from? Was this sound what people had attributed to a baby crying? It appeared to originate from a cluster of trees right along the bank of the creek. I stopped and took several pictures. As I was taking pictures, I noticed a faint red mist forming. I continued to point and shoot with exciting results. As the mist became focused and more defined, it was obvious to me as well as everyone else who was present that it was taking on the shape of a huge circular portal! It was fully formed now, and I could hardly contain my excitement. Then it happened! Orbs began flying out of the center at rapid speeds. I was taken completely by surprise and staggered backward, nearly losing my balance. What the heck was going on? Before long the area was flooded with orbs of every conceivable size and color. Amazing! Cameras were snapping away, and for a time it seemed as if we were caught up in a storm of orbs. Then just as suddenly as they were propelled from the center of the portal, they disappeared from our screens altogether, except for a few stragglers that lingered behind.

What just happened? It was some time before I could fully grasp the meaning of what we had seen. I had of course heard of portals, so the concept was not new to me. However, to see one on my camera screen, to say nothing of watching it form, was exhilarating! Sheer joy gave way to puzzlement, allowing my analytical mind to kick into gear. I was so concerned about losing the photographs that I immediately went to have them removed from my memory card so I could have them in two places, thus ensuring their safety. I think ghost hunters everywhere would agree that to lose a great picture that would offer genuine proof of the existence of portals would be devastating.

Now that they were safely secured, I was able to think about what I had photographed. A portal—most certainly! A great photograph—you bet! Orbs exiting a portal—oh yeah! So what does all this mean in relation to ghosts, other dimensions, and alternate realities? The *what*, *where*, and *when* have been answered, so that only leaves *how* and *why* to explore.

I am sure every devoted ghost enthusiast has wondered at some time or another why some pictures contain so many fantastic orbs. Often they fill the entire screen of digital cameras with mysterious spherical shapes and colors. Could it be that these clusters of orbs have just arrived through a portal via streams of accelerated energy? I believe this is true. Appearing by hundreds, they quickly disappear, floating gracefully toward some unseen destination. Rest assured, if you photograph a cluster of orbs, there is a portal nearby.

Portals are inter-dimensional doorways opening into other realms of existence. Otherworldly dimensions, parallel universes, and the astral world can all be accessed through a portal passageway. Portals are created or brought into being when two or more dimensions or realms of existence overlap each other. This occurrence creates singular inter-dimensional portals whose frequencies blend and form extraordinary structures. They then become fully energized portals in which entities and objects can easily be transported back and forth between dimensions.

The strength of the portal will vary greatly depending on its vibrations and gravitational influence. Any energy form that enters or becomes caught in its electromagnetic field will become transformed and teleportation then becomes possible. This explains how orbs are propelled into our dimension with such ease.

If orbs can be blasted into our realm of existence, one has to wonder who else or what else can also traverse through the use of portals. It's a little scary to think about: aliens, UFOs, reptilians, Yetis, spirit orbs, and who dares to consider what else could be traveling back and forth in this manner.

What about ghost orbs? I believe they are stationary in dimensional frequencies that exist much closer to ours.

Vortexes figure heavily in their appearance and movement within our realm of existence. Other dimensional planes that vibrate at higher frequency levels are invisible to us, yet they too exist. These dimensions have static boundaries that are often experienced by ghost hunters and paranormal investigators who accidentally stumble into them. Those who are sensitive can easily tell when they have reached the outer limits of our reality.

Portals, as dimensional doorways, can open anytime and anywhere. Of course, the most obvious place one would expect to find a portal would be in a cemetery. However, graveyards are a small percentage of the places portals occur. Cemeteries are relatively quiet and offer a place where entities can come and go without disturbing the living, as well as provide very little interference with public activities. Our ancestors probably chose their burial grounds intuitively. Although they made their choices out of necessity, this could have been done either consciously or unconsciously on their part.

In the Victorian age, many large cemeteries resembled parks. They were places where family members gathered to celebrate life and death. They were very picturesque and beautiful. Elaborate tombstones were erected to honor those who had passed on.

The question often arises as to why ghosts would be found in a cemetery. When and if they are photographed there, it is probably because they seek to communicate with the living. They remember those who come to pay their respects, and they seek to gain their attention. Of course if they encounter someone who is clairvoyant or clairaudient, they revel in trying to relay messages. They may also be attracted to ghost hunters because of their electrical equipment and, being curious, find ways to get their attention. They have come into contact with someone who acknowledges their presence and may respond to requests to appear in photographs.

Cemeteries offering passages to heavenly dimensions were often placed close to churches, rivers, and streams, as well as unseen portals, again either intuitively or unconsciously, to aid spirit in its quest for immortality.

American Indians, medicine men, and shamans were very astute at choosing burial grounds as spiritual sites to elevate their loved ones to higher dimensions. Their innate sense of nature and spiritual vibrations allowed them to choose places where portals may have been for centuries. These sites were revered by Indian nations and superstitiously avoided by less evolved individuals who dared not enter these sacred grounds for fear of retribution. Sacred sites usually have an otherworldly feel about them. Many old cemeteries, whose auras are sensed as eerie or extremely peaceful, may be hot spots for activity.

How can you tell if you are in close proximity to a phenomenal portal? There are several telltale signs. Landscapes may appear shady or unnaturally light. These areas will be inconsistent with the natural surroundings. Vaguely discernible outlines, especially in deep foliage or against a scenic background, are also clues to a portal's existence. There may be a faint energy field much like a mirage between an investigator and objects to be photographed. Always pay close attention to mysterious mists or fogs that appear out of nowhere and become concentrated and localized.

Look for odd light configurations such as bright luminous rods, streaks, orbs, or spherical shapes of dense light moving at rapid speeds. Any number of anomalous forms may appear from a seemingly calm area, streaking along at incredible speeds and leaving a noticeable contrail behind them.

Audible noises similar to humming or low-key buzzing sounds may be heard as the portal opens and closes. They may sound far away, but could in reality be very nearby. Any odd or unusual sensations could also indicate the nearness of a dimensional portal. There may be static electricity in the area around a portal. There may also be a transference of energies, whether it be etheric or from higher frequencies, that could produce communication with otherworldly beings.

You may be witness to physical objects appearing near you on the ground. These items did not just go unnoticed by you—they were not there before! Crystals, arrowheads, feathers, jewelry, and many other apports (solid objects believed to be teleported from another dimension) have been suddenly discovered lying near portals, although nothing was seen at the time. I can assure you that the rain did not wash them up nor did the wind blow them there, and the ground did not simply unearth them. They landed there or were placed there from within the portal. Any form of matter that is synonymous with both dimensions is able to interconnect and teleport between the two dimensions.

One sign that there is an influx of new energies is that one's ears may begin to ring ever so lightly. The sound may then rise sharply. When our body's energy receptors interact with unfamiliar frequencies, there will be a state of either harmony or discord. People who are sensitive to different energy patterns may experience these energies in either one or more of the following ways:

DISCORDANT ENERGY

Energy drain	Nausea
Inability to move	Disorientation
Weakness	Confusion
Cold chills	Headaches
Vertigo	Feelings of being watched

On the positive side, many psychics and clairvoyants, as well as others, experience pleasant harmonious energies at sacred sites, such as the following:

HARMONIOUS ENERGY

Mental clarity	Increased energy
Euphoria	Feelings of protection
Calmness	Happiness
Peace	Elation

Portals are not limited to outside areas only. They may also occur within the walls of any structure, natural or man-made, even caves and tunnels. In structures, look for sudden unexplained appearances of shadow silhouettes, apparitions, or unexpected mists that appear seemingly out of nowhere.

Listen for disembodied voices as well as the sound of suspicious footsteps that come and go periodically.

Sometimes the efusal of a pet to enter a room or an animal behaving strangely could indicate portal activity. Animals vibrate at higher frequencies than humans; this often allows them to see and hear through dimensions much more easily than we can. It's always a good idea to pay attention to their reaction to any phenomena.

Pay attention to your intuition. If you feel or get a sense of an invisible opening in perhaps a closet, basement, attic, or a particular room, you may not be imagining things, especially if you feel tingling sensations when approaching that area.

I would like to add a word of caution. You may indirectly use thoughts and words that raise your level of consciousness to the exact frequency of a parallel dimension, thereby opening a portal. You should *never* try to do so purposely. Once you experience a door to the other side, you will never be able to pretend it doesn't exist. Your concept of time and space will be altered, and your logical mind will begin to question the linear sequence of time, demanding you acknowledge past, present, and future as one.

We have planned a full investigation of "Cry-Baby-Creek" in the fall when pleasant weather will enhance our efforts. Hot Texas summers, mosquitoes, and bats can put a damper on even the most ardent ghost hunter.

Please take portals seriously, even if you are a ghost hunter or paranormal investigator. Always expect the unexpected!

THIRTEEN

ENERGY ANOMALIES

I existed from all eternity and, behold, I am here;
and I shall exist till the end of time,
for my being has no end.

KAHLIL GIBRAN (1883–1931)

A very interesting anomaly has been photographed repeatedly by members of our team, and although of unknown origin, it as been given many names: light rods, speeders, streaks, ribbons, and squiggles, to name a few. While a clear definition eludes most ghost hunters, we all agree that they are very impressive when caught on film as they streak by. Although they are not seen with the naked eye, they appear on too many photographs to be ignored.

Their basic shape is long and narrow, but here the similarities end. They have been photographed as swirling, bending, wiggling, and in all manner of shapes. They may appear segmented or with a snakelike head effect at the front of the long, luminous beam of light. I have personally photographed hundreds of these, and I am very intrigued by their ability to form letters. I have captured the initials to my name as well as many other letters. This leads me to believe that they are intelligent energy sources that are seeking to communicate with us. These perceived lines of energy seem to create specific patterns. I feel that these are symbolic messages in and of themselves.

They may be photographed as brilliant solitary streaks or they may be traveling in groups. They may also appear as a mass of intertwined energy ropes that are awesome to look at. These oddities seem to be found more in cemeteries than anywhere else, but as is true with all anomalies, they can be found just about anywhere.

They have been photographed inside as well as outside. They are found and photographed everywhere there are people. These luminous streaks of light have been photographed in many old buildings and cemeteries.

They are often referred to as "energized orbs" by paranormal investigators and ghost hunters alike. However, they differ from orbs in several ways. They appear much brighter and more intensely illuminated. We've even referred to them as "neon snakes." These bedazzling spirit lights show up in photographs as bright neon colors: red, orange, green, blue, yellow, and hot pink. These intensely vibrant colors are an indication of a much stronger vibrational frequency that is consistent with highly evolved souls or spirit beings.

Spirits that are not earthbound are able to visit us and make their presence known. They are able to shift their vibrational frequency to synchronize with ours, thus allowing us to perceive them. As spirits, they enter our dimension at an accelerated rate of speed, often leaving a contrail of light behind them.

Spirits from other dimensions are invisible to us. However, those who exist in other dimensions are very aware of us. They are able to interact with consistency, although we are not often aware of their visitations.

So, what do I believe? I believe that these peculiar glowing streaks of light-consciousness are spirits who are highly evolved. I do not think that they are ghosts, or at least not as I perceive ghosts to be. Simply put, I believe that these luminous beams of light, being photographed all over the world, are spirit manifesting in its purest form.

When I was much younger and just beginning to acknowledge my gifts of clairvoyance and clairaudience, I would go through hours of question-and-answer sessions with my guides. I was wildly curious about everything related to my guides and angels including how it was possible for them to communicate with me. Questions about how and where they existed were always on my mind.

I remember that one of the questions I asked most often was: "Who are you, really?" My guides always answered my questions the same way. "We are flowing streams of energy." I recall thinking, what an odd statement. I could not exactly relate to them due to my youth and inexperience. I had not gained the spiritual awareness I needed to elevate me to that level of understanding. So I just conceptualized them as I perceived them in dreams and sporadic visions. They appeared as "Allie," an older wise female, and "Woody," a young witty male and an Englishman to boot! Obviously they encouraged my perception of them as a nonthreatening way of presenting themselves to me. It would have been hard for me to relate to them as "flowing streams of energy consciousness" at such a young age. Now however, especially as I see them as such, it is very easy for me to understand their messages. Hopefully, someday soon I will be able to discern the message of the symbolic patterns, letters, and colors they project as they streak in and out of our dimension.

We are entering an age of new awareness, higher technology, spiritual acceptance, and occult understanding. I believe that being able to photograph unseen energies is only the beginning of a new dimension of spirituality. To me, a photograph is the closest thing to physical proof that invisible intelligences exist. Seeing is believing, after all.

I do believe that spirits as well as ghosts are using our advanced technology as a way to contact us. I think the message we receive through photography is that they are aware of us, they can and do interact with us, and they have information that they want to share. They are attempting to guide us by expanding our awareness of other realms of existence. We are all multidimensional beings, and as such we should be able to accept consciously our unlimited ability to perceive alternate realities.

If you capture luminous energy as streaks of light, segmented ropelike images, rods, or squiggles, look and listen for a message, especially if you are presented with a neon representation of your initial or name.

Based on my clairvoyant perception and paranormal experiences, I would define these light anomalies as pure spirit energy. I also believe that this strong energy is capable of presenting itself as solid spirit beings, angels, and human forms that appear as normal as you and I do. So when they start to show up in your photographs, intensify your awareness of your surroundings, as you may be witness to an apparition in its most glorified form.

FOURTEEN

WHO ARE GHOST HUNTERS, ANYWAY?

We don't see things as they are; we see them as we are!

ANAÏS NIN (1903–1977)

Ghost Hunters—Paranormal Researchers—Spirit Investigators. Who are they? Where do they come from? Why do they hunt ghosts anyway? What is the point? These are good questions and I have great answers.

They are normal people just like you and me. They work, live, and play all around us. They hunt ghosts because they know deep in their souls that ghosts are real and that they coexist with us in this dimension. For the most part, ghost hunters are dedicated people from all walks of life who put a lot of time and energy into the research and investigation of paranormal events. They seek to discover verifiable evidence that ghosts are real. They uncover and expose what is hidden by ignorance, offering real proof of life beyond death. Yes, ghosts do exist!

A ghost hunter can be just about anyone. They work as teachers, reporters, psychics, nurses, carpenters, plumbers, authors, bartenders, clerks, housewives, roofers, psychologists, lawyers—almost every conceivable field may have ghost hunters working day-by-day right alongside everyone else. They can be family members, friends, and even your next door neighbor.

Are they evil, weird, scary, threatening, or dangerous? Certainly not! Are they interesting, dedicated, understanding, and exciting? Yes, they are!

Most ghost hunters are eager to explain what they do and how they do it. They respect themselves and each other and are not easily affected by the skeptics who so often debunk their investigative research methods. They are community-oriented and most will eagerly donate their time and effort to community projects such as cemetery restoration and the preservation of historical sites and old buildings.

Ghost hunters usually become a part of an existing group, a team member, or they may form their own organization in an attempt to document, record, and photograph paranormal phenomena that will support the existence of ghosts.

Discarnate souls are always near us; it is only our perception of them that prevents us from accepting them as they really are. Their realm interpenetrates ours and they exist at a different vibrational frequency than we do.

As a group or team, ghost hunters create a support system to help keep each other motivated and also to back them up when faced with harsh criticism from die-hard skeptics. I think that most skeptics really want to believe. However, they have been conditioned from childhood to believe that there is no such thing as ghosts. Of course, they have no alternative but to say that ghosts are simply figments of an overactive imagination. They willingly try to discredit photographic evidence by saying it is dust, lens flare, moisture, fog, smoke, or other mundane examples of nature.

What most skeptics do not seem to realize is that ghost hunters are often their own worst critics. They know their equipment and the results it produces; they honestly acknowledge their own emotional, physical, and intuitive reactions to paranormal events; and willingly offer up evidence to other team members for serious study and scrutiny. If a piece of evidence passes the team's criteria for ghostly phenomena, they then offer it for public review.

What you will see are their experiences, research abilities, and personal knowledge of paranormal phenomena combined with factual evidence. This combination will offer genuine proof that we coexist with ghosts and spirits on a daily basis.

It's impossible for anyone to declare that they are an expert when it comes to investigating paranormal phenomena. It's a controversial field cluttered with more questions than answers. A lot of information is based on theories alone due to the fact that science is unable to prove the validity of ghosts.

For a ghost hunter, researcher, or investigator to fully understand paranormal events and even ghosts themselves, it is essential for them to evaluate these unseen energies from a human perspective. Why? Because ghosts were alive at one time; they lived, breathed, worked, and played just as you and I do today. Although invisible to us now, they are still capable of exhibiting personalities and emotions just as they did when they were alive.

When ghosts are active, they are only seeking attention. They want to be acknowledged. They may become upset or even angry when you fail to recognize them or respond to their attempts at communication. Perhaps they are not able to interact with us as they wish to. When these events unfold, they usually generate enough energy to create events and ghostly manifestations that may force homeowners and confused individuals to seek help.

ENTER THE GHOST HUNTER

At this point, a ghost hunter or paranormal investigator is usually called in to help figure out what is causing the disturbance and who or what is creating it. Investigators act as detectives to determine the source of the ghostly manifestations presented to them. They respond as counselors while interviewing the homeowner or client to get a clear picture of what is really going on. They listen to their stories and complaints and are careful not to jump to conclusions about a suspected event.

Educating the home owner or client is a big part of the initial interview. Explaining what it may or may not be often helps them understand the situation. They will not feel as alone in their dilemma, and as ghost hunters, we can validate them by our presence and perhaps even ease their fear of "going crazy."

Regardless of what you have heard, seen on television, or perceived on your own, ghost hunters do not just play around with high-tech equipment. They put a tremendous amount of time and energy as well as a lot of themselves into any investigation. I believe that most ghost hunters will agree that an investigator's true reward comes from helping alleviate someone's fear of death and ghosts, as well as eerie ghostly phenomena.

What movies and television portray as a ghostly presence is not an accurate account of the true identity of ghosts. It simply must not be relied on as the truth. I can assure you that it is a gross exaggeration in regard to the reality of ghosts.

Most ghost hunters, as a team or group, do not charge for an investigation. However, if the location is a considerable distance away, food, travel, and overnight lodging costs will need to be allowed for. Therefore donations are willingly accepted to help offset these expenses.

Ghost hunters are dedicated to research, documentation, and education about ghosts and spirits. If you believe you are being haunted, have a ghost in your home, or are experiencing ghostly activity in any of its various forms, get in touch with a well-known, reputable ghost-hunting organization. They can help!

They will conduct a formal investigation of your home, office, structure, or any location where they are needed. They will be able to confirm or deny your suspicions and discuss your fears free of charge, most of the time. Ghosts are considered paranormal only because they are an extraordinary example of something that is beyond your normal perception of reality.

So, who are ghost hunters? They are people who can help you regain your power by sharing their knowledge of what they do. They will help you embrace the unknown; they can help you understand what you are dealing with, no matter how scary it may appear on the surface. They can close the gap between religion, culture, and metaphysical concepts to assist you in understanding ghosts.

Remember, if you have a question, ask. Ghost hunters may just have the answer you have been looking for.

FIFTEEN

INVESTIGATIONS
AND FIELD TRIPS

Ancestors are still in our midst,
appearing at times as light spheres.

<small>CARL JUNG</small> (1875–1961)

Okay, so I've piqued your interest, and you would like to try your hand at ghost hunting. Great!

One of the first things you can do to develop your skill as a paranormal ghost hunter is to go on an investigation with a reputable ghost-hunting organization. Going out on field trips or investigations for experience and relaxation can be a lot of fun, as well as very educational. Ghost-hunting groups vary in size, protocol, and professionalism, so choosing a team that is right for each person is very important. A group or team that is knowledgeable and enthusiastic can enhance your ability to become a credible ghost hunter. Some groups may come from a fun, thrill-seeking stance, others from a spiritual or metaphysical outlook, and others still from a very serious research agenda.

I really enjoy our investigative team because we encompass so many different personalities, viewpoints, and ideas. Each team member brings into the group their own personal concepts of ghosts and paranormal phenomena, which is very enlightening.

Not every investigation has to be so serious that you lose sight of the very thing you are investigating. It is much better to be lighthearted, relaxed, and inquisitive. When choosing a group or selecting a team, pick people who are easy to get along with and people who relate to each other easily. There is really no room for self-centered egotism in ghost hunting; everyone should be willing to accept each other's advice. Look, learn, listen, and always trust your own intuition. This will help a group to become a successful, respected investigative team. No one person knows everything. I learn something new every time we go on an investigation or field trip. Every investigation is different and filled with new evidence to be explored and documented.

I mention field trips as well as investigations as they are two entirely different things, yet similar in many ways.

FIELD TRIPS

Is the team bored? No investigations pending? Go on a field trip! It's great fun to visit cemeteries, battlefields, haunted hotels, and just about anywhere that would be suitable for a group or several team members to go together. Our group recently went to a reportedly haunted hotel in Jefferson, Texas. It was relaxing and fun and only a short distance away. We explored the history of the town, stayed all night in the famed haunted Jefferson Hotel, and took photographs in a wonderful cemetery in a neighboring town— all with exciting, unexpected results.

Although we expected to get orbs in our photos, we never expected to capture a Civil War apparition, but that is exactly what happened! He was photographed in the most unlikely place, near an old abandoned warehouse. We were thrilled with the outcome of our trip and everyone had a great time.

Field trips can be refreshing, highly motivating, and rewarding as well. So when things slow down and there seems to be nothing going on, create a ghost hunt. There is always somewhere to go, something to explore, history to be uncovered, and one never knows where or when a ghostly presence might be encountered.

When traveling with a group, it is helpful to follow a few rules or at least a well-defined plan. Have everyone meet at a designated place and either carpool or follow the leader. This prevents a lot of confusion as everyone arrives together and no one gets lost. It also makes it a lot easier when it comes to checking into hotels, as everyone is accounted for.

We usually appoint a specific team member (it doesn't always have to be the same person) as our public relations person. That person is responsible for talking to anyone who wants to ask questions about our group's activities such as reporters, the curious public in general, or even police officers. It is always a good habit to try to blend in with other tourists or the local community. I always try to avoid people who draw attention to themselves or do things that are contradictory to my purpose. I love the ambiance of old cemeteries, old towns, and historical settings, and I hate to see this disrupted by people who do not understand how conducive these places are to ghost hunts.

I always carry a small notebook with me on field trips to jot down notes of things as they happen, especially if they are unique or unexpected events. It also serves as a journal of my trip and provides me with information that I might otherwise have forgotten.

Because we visit historical sites and public places, we are always careful not to trespass. We make a point of asking permission before breaking out our cameras and recorders. This is just common courtesy, and we want to be respected for our ethical standards. Most of the people we encounter are interested in what we do, which often leads to future investigations. People almost always point out other places for us to investigate, which can be very rewarding. They seem to enjoy sharing stories, rumors, and legends about haunted places. This helps to keep us motivated and keeps our calendar filled with ghost-hunting activities.

Basically, field trips give us an opportunity to explore places that have never been investigated before. Of course, it is always fun to check out reported paranormal phenomena and ghostly activity at well-known sites that may be nearby.

Field trips give us a chance to record, film, and document new evidence for our organization and the public in general. Information gathered as evidence of ghosts can be used for many additional things, such as writing articles, giving workshops, or creating a film documentary.

Many ghost hunters, while having fun, have stumbled upon new directions in life, especially when spirit was directing them unawares. In my opinion, when it comes to evidence, enough is *never* enough! Field trips are fun. Plan one soon!

INVESTIGATIONS

A formal investigation is a well-planned research and documentation process. The team members are dedicated to finding the source of a paranormal disturbance and understanding why it is happening.

Investigations involve several techniques and procedures that must be followed to retain the team's integrity. Investigations should always begin with an interview. When conducting an interview, we may be talking to someone who is distraught, scared, confused, or just plain weird. Whatever the case, we are persistent with our questions, taking note of any unusual comments made by family members or others who are present. Their responses may be clues that will help us determine what is going on. We look for repeated statements and make mental notes as we gather information. We are aware that as we play the roles of detective, confidant, and counselor, we need to trust our intuition. Before the interview is over, we will probably have a pretty good idea of what is creating the disturbance.

After the interview is complete, we provide beneficial information to the homeowner or client. We explain what equipment we will be using and how it will help during the investigation. Finally, we discuss a time and date for a full investigation. We determine who will be present and discuss any areas that will be off-limits to the team. We strive to always perform our research and investigations in a professional manner. This is essential to a group's integrity.

Probably the most disliked part of ghost hunting, however, is also one of the most important: written documentation. We begin our written accounts by listing the team members who are present and will participate in the investigation. We always list the person's name and also their particular interest or specialty, such as photography, electronic voice phenomena (EVP), or the use of scanning equipment such as electromagnetic field detectors (EMF), as well as thermal heat sensors. It's interesting to note that sometimes a team member will decide to try something different, such as using the digital recorder instead of the camera, and, guess what, they get an EVP. Was this a coincidence? Absolutely not! They were being led by spirit and directed to use that particular tool in order to communicate with unseen energies. This happens quite often in our group, so we are getting used to it and staying more flexible with our tools. If one tool is not producing the desired effect and one of us feels drawn toward another tool, it just might produce surprising results.

The next entry is the date and time of arrival, along with the address of the location. Here we also list all structures on the property at the time of the investigation or draw a little map of the area. We also take note of any buildings that used to be on the property, such as slave quarters, sheds, warehouses, barns, or storage buildings. Also, and this is very important, we ask if there are any graves located on the property. Although the paranormal disturbance may be in the house or a building, it could be generated from outside.

An ad placed in the local newspaper landed us a fortunate investigation at an old antebellum house that was built sometime in the late 1830s. During the course of the investigation, we began to notice that there appeared to be an incredible amount of activity outside the house. Further research revealed that four family members and possibly more were buried on the grounds. Broken tombstones were found inside a shed at the back of the house, and the orb activity increased the longer we stayed outside. Although paranormal activity was documented inside the house, it was increasingly obvious to all team members that the unsettling disturbance was coming from a source outside the house. Giving careful consideration to the outside surroundings in an investigation may provide additional clues to a paranormal disturbance.

The next important entry should be notes regarding the weather conditions at the time of the investigation. Record the temperature both inside and outside the house or structure upon arrival. Note any precipitation such as rain, snow, or fog. Unusual atmospheric activity, such as an approaching storm, strong wind gusts, or lightning, should also be taken into account.

Here are some examples of basic rules and procedures that you may want to follow to ensure a successful investigation.

Never ghost hunt alone! This should be everyone's number one rule. For safety reasons, we need the company of our fellow team members or friends who share our ghost-hunting enthusiasm. Secondly, we want to have additional witnesses to any paranormal activity we may encounter.

Recently a friend of mine called me on her cell phone from a nearby, long-forgotten old cemetery. She sounded a little apprehensive as she was telling me about what had just happened to her while she was alone in the cemetery. She unlocked her car doors and they would immediately lock right back! This happened so many times that she decided (and rightfully so) to leave the cemetery. After discussing the event, we decided to go back together to try to determine what was happening. We did just that, except this time there were three of us: my friend, my ten-year–old ghost-hunting granddaughter, and me. Shortly after we arrived, the same activity began anew. We would unlock the doors and within minutes they would lock right back. Not only did the doors lock repeatedly, but the car's alarm started to go off. We looked around for any electrical source that could be accidentally affecting the car's system, but could find nothing. The cemetery is in a rural country area and well hidden. While we were there, we were able to photograph collaborating evidence to add validity to the activity we experienced.

She was using her Sony digital camera and my granddaughter and I had our Kodak digitals with us. We were both drawn to a specific area of the cemetery, and simultaneously we snapped our cameras. We both photographed a huge, deep-blue orb midway between the ground and an old tree. It was about two o'clock in the afternoon, and we were really surprised to capture a daytime orb of this size and texture. Even my granddaughter photographed an area with dense ecto-mist. Although we did not tarry long, we do plan to go back with our team for a full investigation. We are in the process of researching to find out as much as possible about this eerie cemetery. Some people we have talked to believe it could have been an old slave cemetery, but that remains to be authenticated.

Will my friend ever go out alone again? I don't believe she will! She has learned her lesson well. Experience really is the best teacher!

Never trespass. Always ask permission. I can't stress this enough. This is an extremely important issue and should never be neglected. We always carry proper identification, including business cards, in case we are approached by members of law enforcement agencies. This indicates that we are not loitering and that we are serious about paranormal research.

Also, we never smoke on an investigation. This prevents confusion when reviewing photographs. A skeptic's favorite response in regard to ecto-mist is "smoke"! We also never drink while on site. Drinking dulls one's senses and we need to be as alert as possible. We have to pay attention to what we are feeling, hearing, seeing, and sensing. Our senses are finely tuned tools, and we want to be able to use them effectively.

In cold weather, we always try to hold our breath as we snap a picture to prevent confusion as to what was captured on film. Breath exhaled when it is cold will appear as ecto-mist on photographs. So we got into the habit of holding our breath just long enough to snap the shutter, and it has become second nature to do it that way, thus eliminating yet another favorite skeptical response: "breath."

Never take photographs in rainy or snowy weather. Here again, we don't want to give the skeptics something else to call "raindrops" or "snow."

Take along a first-aid kit. As an amateur ghost hunter, I remember thinking, "Oh, I will never use that." Well, I can assure you that at some point it will be needed. Surprisingly, unexpected things happen all the time on ghost hunts, and it is better to be prepared than regret it later.

Wear comfortable clothing and sturdy shoes. The ghosts couldn't care less what we are wearing, and we want to be as comfortable as possible. Sturdy shoes or boots are my favorites because we never know where we will be walking or what we will be walking into.

Take along snacks and water; we have to keep ourselves energized. Fresh fruit is always a good bet, as are power drinks such as Gatorade. We always take along a trash bag and pick up any trash generated by our team, often leaving an area cleaner than we found it.

Last, but certainly not least: no horseplay allowed! No running is allowed, and never, under any circumstances, does anyone attempt to scare people! This is definitely not acceptable.

Finally, when I begin an investigation, I always talk calmly to any unseen ghosts or spirits who may be there. I explain what we are doing, why we are there, and ask them to respond in a positive, benevolent manner. A lot of them do not realize that their presence is frightening to others. I always thank them for sharing their space with us and proceed with the investigation. This process will often open doors to active communication, allowing us to get better pictures, record clearer EVPs, and also witness some pretty incredible paranormal phenomena.

After an investigation is over, we usually head straight for the nearest restaurant, truck stop, or all-night grill to relax and discuss our investigation. Orange juice really seems to restore my depleted energy, and as for food, who can pass that up? We never draw conclusions immediately after an investigation, reserving our opinions about our observations until all the evidence has been reviewed. Then a comprehensive written report is compiled along with any photographs or other evidence that was documented and given to the homeowner or client.

As we depart for the last time, we thank the client for the shared opportunity to assist them in their time of need, as well as the experience we gained as a result of the investigation. This may lead to new investigations and will most certainly help us retain our ethical standards and credibility as ghost hunters.

We also keep in mind that experience is the best teacher, and even if our investigation did not reveal anything out of the ordinary, our time was not wasted. We never know *who* or *what* was watching us! Ghosts and spirits are only a vibration away from us. They can be with us instantly by merely thinking about us. Just because they might not have shown themselves at that particular time does not mean that they were not there. They may have chosen to wait instead until a more appropriate time to contact us. They may present themselves at a repeat visit or they may not.

The field of ghost hunting is exciting and offers many spiritual rewards to those who are willing to experience vibrational energies in new ways.

SIXTEEN

A GHOST HUNTER'S TOOL KIT

If a man harbors any sort of fear,
it makes him landlord to a ghost.

LLOYD DOUGLAS (1893–1975)

Before I begin to write about the various tools that can be used for accumulating useful information in an investigation, I would like to point out what I believe is the most important tool of all. This tool is free, uses no batteries, is always available, and is of major importance in the field as well as in frightening situations. This tool is you!

The information you gather and how it is recorded depends upon your ability to override emotion, think clearly, and, last but not least, interpret your own intuitive perception. What is really going on during an investigation can only be thoroughly accessed by using your innate and perhaps latent spiritual gifts. As you ask yourself the *who, how,* and *why* questions, you will be touching higher realms of spiritual awareness.

Being clairvoyant as well as clairaudient, I can easily testify to the fact that psychics are a strong asset to any investigation, whether it is ghost hunting or the more traditional detective investigations. I can't imagine why many investigators and researchers refuse to use them on their teams. Perhaps they have not dealt with their own personal fears of the unknown. Whatever the reason, it is clear that sensitive investigators and psychics can and do make worthwhile contributions to ghost hunting and paranormal research.

Many psychics can communicate with ghosts, supplying the team with information about the haunting. They can express emotions and relay messages, helpful insights, and even names and dates that could not be known in any other way.

I know that everyone has their own personal level of psychic ability or "special gifts," if you feel more comfortable with that term. Perhaps the only difference is that most empowered psychics grew up in homes where paranormal happenings were commonplace. They probably had people in their lives who taught them how to develop their gifts as well as how to use them. They were introduced to their gifts at an early age and therefore had no reason to fear them or the mysterious universe we live in.

If you are fortunate enough to have a gifted psychic on your team as an investigator, friend, or just someone who comes along out of curiosity, they should be treated just like everyone else. I can assure you they will be very appreciative of this.

They understand possibly more than most that everyone has a job to do and that each person there is equally important.

Psychics have been used in many highly respected fields, such as law enforcement, the medical field, huge corporations, and the military, not to mention covert government operations. So why not ghost research? An experienced psychic can be a valuable asset to your team, and as you are entering the realm of the unknown, you should be open to all forms of paranormal assistance. I feel that researchers and investigators should not ignore anything that would help them validate their efforts, especially since skeptics are so eager to discredit their evidence.

As an investigator, you can easily rely on your own intuition to enhance your ability to take photographs, record

EVPs, and document valuable information. Pay close attention to your feelings, listen to your inner voice, and *never* second-guess your first impressions, especially when entering a building for the first time.

If you sense something around or near you, take a picture in that direction. Some of my most prized photographs have been obtained in this manner. If an area of a room or a particular part of a building keeps drawing your attention, set up your recording equipment there. Video cameras, EVP recorders, and infrared still cameras may produce exciting results in these areas.

Ghosts are attracted to investigators with whom they resonate, those whose vibrational frequencies are compatible to their own unique vibrations. Pay attention to your senses: hearing, sight, smell, emotional responses, and gut instincts. By using these senses, you can enhance your ability to document fantastic paranormal activity.

Before we explore the traditional tools used for ghost hunting, I would like to share one of my investigative secrets with you. You are probably aware that quartz is the material from which crystal balls are formed. But did you know that even small pieces of quartz crystals have paranormal properties and uses as well? Quartz acts as an amplifier of energy and enhances vibrational frequencies as well as all forms of communication. Crystals strengthen the connection between spiritual dimensions and enable their users to make contact with ghosts and spirits.

Because crystals act as a channel for psychic energies, wearing crystal jewelry or carrying a small crystal will raise your awareness and enhance your vibrational perception. To activate your crystal, you will need to wear it or carry it on you for at least one week. This allows the crystal to attune to your own personal vibrational frequency.

Crystals can also deflect negative energies. Your crystal can cleanse your immediate environment by dispelling unacceptable energies from the building, house, or site you are investigating.

The shape of the crystal has no effect on its paranormal abilities. You can use natural quartz or refined quartz. It can be shaped as a pendant, a small figure, or any unique shape that appeals to you. It is, however, important to remember that you do not choose the crystal, it chooses you! By the same standard, if a crystal suddenly shows up in your life, comes to you as a gift, a lucky find, or otherwise mysteriously appears, it has chosen you. If this happens during an investigation or while on a field trip, be aware that you are being led to investigate deeper into the ghostly realm for a specific reason.

INVESTIGATIVE TOOLS

I don't believe that there is any such thing as unnatural or occult phenomena. Although a rare event, the very fact that something odd or unusual happens makes it natural. It is simply unexplained paranormal (beyond normal) phenomena. Just because you experience unusual manifestations of energy without warning does not mean that it's not a normal function of energy.

Ghostly phenomena are puzzling, to say the least. Ghosts cause energy disturbances by using existing energy sources to manifest mysterious forms and phenomenal anomalies. These often unexplainable energy patterns offer genuine evidence of ghostly contact.

A lack of form does not necessarily mean that something does not exist. Energy has its own unique form of consciousness; *never doubt this*. Everything also has its own distinct vibration. These vibrations reveal how that particular energy manifests, as well as clues to its energized form.

Unrelated to visions and audible sound, the subtlest form of communication is conveyed by energy frequencies that transmit information and knowledge to those who willingly seek contact. This communication can come to you as symbols, synchronistic events, and coincidences. Be open to all forms of communication and try to discern the messages.

How do we locate ghosts? How do we know when they are in close proximity to us? How do we communicate with them? If we have not fully developed our psychic awareness (I say "fully developed" because I believe that we are all in varying stages of spiritual development), then we must rely on the investigative tools of the trade.

The first ghost hunters had to rely entirely on their intuitive abilities to communicate with spirits and ghosts. They did not have the fancy technical equipment and intriguing gadgets that are available to ghost hunters today. They relied on their own innate intuition and perhaps primitive tools such as dowsing rods (which, by the way, work very well, even today). Ghosts are seen, voices are heard, and questions need to be answered. Today's equipment, coupled with investigative skills, offers exciting and often shocking results when exposing ghostly activities.

Every piece of equipment in a ghost hunter's tool kit is capable of providing evidence for the existence of ghosts. More advanced tools and newer technology help to document ghosts, giving the die-hard skeptics less and less power to dispute their existence.

Researchers need to be familiar with their equipment. I highly recommend that you practice using your equipment in total darkness. The first time I heard this, I laughed out loud. Well, guess what? The joke was on me. If you cannot effectively turn your equipment on, change your batteries, or adjust the settings on your equipment in the dark, you will lose valuable time and maybe even the chance of a lifetime to record something unique, like the "holy grail" of any investigation, a full apparition! Experience is the best teacher, and I certainly had to learn the hard way. So practice using your camera, recorders, video equipment, and digital devices in the dark. You will be glad you did. Experimenting with your equipment could mean the difference between wasted investigations or great results with excellent usable evidence.

Ghosts emit electromagnetic energy. Successful investigations depend upon your ability to detect these energies using your technical equipment as tools, thereby enhancing your chances of proving the existence of ghosts.

Cameras
Of all the traditional tools, the camera is possibly the oldest and still one of the most prolific ghost-hunting tools on the

market today. Cameras were probably the first supportive pieces of equipment used in ghost hunting. Indeed, they gained popularity during the Victorian era due to spirit photography. Introduced by a Boston engraver named William H. Mumler in 1862 were photographs that contained ghosts, apparitions, and spirit images. News of his uncanny ability to capture ghosts on film soon spread like wildfire and opened a new era of ghost photography. Spirit photography had enormous appeal during the Civil War. Bereaved families sought tangible proof to assure them that their loved ones continued to exist even after death. Spirit photography gave them the proof they so desperately needed.

A camera is one of the most important tools for an investigator. Almost any kind of camera will work and it does not have to be expensive to be efficient. Even handy disposable cameras, as well as Polaroids, can capture and reveal ghostly anomalies. Don't be intimidated if all you have to start with is a film camera. Everyone has to start somewhere. Some of my best pictures were taken with a disposable camera. You can always add supportive evidence from other equipment (which again does not have to be expensive) to add validity to your photographic evidence.

Film Camera

At one time, the most widely used cameras were 35-mm cameras chosen over older film models and Polaroids. Film cameras are still widely in use and have their plus sides for ghost hunting. On the upside, with a film camera you will have the negative to back up your photographs, and this seems to be extremely important to die-hard skeptics who analyze everything to death. With a negative, you can send your photograph along with the negative to the film manufacturer and ask for their opinion as to what is on the film. You will receive an official response from professionals, which will either validate your perceptions or explain exactly what caused the image, such as a lens flare, double exposure, or bad film, for example. On the downside, there is the cost of film with the added expense of processing. Developing film takes time, and as any investigator knows, it is hard to wait to see the results of your efforts. There is of course the off chance that you will have an entire roll of film without any positive results and this can be very disappointing. However, with this in mind when I use a film camera, I always try to position people, other investigators, unique tombstones, and points of interest in my pictures so that if I'm not lucky enough to capture a ghost or an anomaly I still have valuable photos.

Shadow ghosts are notorious for appearing behind people, objects, and tombstones, so look closely for these in your pictures. I use 400-speed film for daytime photos and highly recommend higher speeds for evening and nighttime shots. Kodak Royal Gold 1000-speed film is especially good for outdoor shots and after-dark photography. Some ghost hunters experiment with infrared film; however, this is not as cost-efficient as other affordable film that works just as well.

It is also very important to let the developer know that you want *all* of your pictures, especially the bad ones. The photographs that appear damaged or out of focus could just be your best shots. A film developer will not recognize orbs, ecto-mist, or a fuzzy apparition, so remember to ask for all photos to be returned to you.

Polaroids

While Polaroids are great for instant results, the price of the film is expensive. They do, however, work well for capturing ghosts and unseen energies such as unusual ecto-mist, unique vortexes, shadow ghosts, and orbs.

My brother Ricky Joe gets exciting pictures with his Polaroid camera. On a recent field trip to a local cemetery, he was able to photograph two very interesting anomalies. He collects clocks as a hobby, and it seems that someone or something wanted him to know that they knew that this was his passion. As he was passing under a huge oak tree, he suddenly felt compelled to take a picture upward into the tree. It was the last picture he had, so he snapped, expecting nothing more than leaves and branches. We were all amazed at what we saw as we watched it develop. Two huge yellow orbs appeared. Of course we had all seen a lot of orbs on many different ghost hunts and investigations; however, what was unique about these two orbs was that they both had clock faces on them. The clock faces were very plain: the hands on the first orb were pointing to two o'clock, the exact time we arrived at the cemetery, and the other clock face pointed to five-fifteen, the exact time that the photograph was taken. Amazing! I think it goes without saying that Ricky Joe is very proud of his unique photograph.

Digital Camera

Digital cameras are great tools for the research and investigation of paranormal phenomena. The digital age has introduced many new and innovative cameras. In an effort to prove conclusively that ghosts exist, investigators often rely on the latest technology.

There are many advantages to using digital cameras; the cost of the film is eliminated, you don't have to wait to get your pictures back, and you don't have to pay developing fees. However you must purchase a memory card, which is a one-time expense. I consider this a small price to pay for all the added benefits.

If there is a downside to digital photography, it would be that it does not supply you with a negative. There is no way to prove that a photo was not manipulated with software programs used for creative endeavors.

When analyzing your photographs, enlargements often need to be made for closer viewing. With digital photography, enlargements may sometimes appear grainy. To eliminate this problem, set your camera to its highest quality setting. While this may reduce the number of pictures your memory card will hold, it enhances the probability of excellent enlargements.

Many people wonder why digital cameras seem to be able to capture ghostly anomalies better and clearer than other cameras. I was also curious, so I researched how they work. In a nutshell, when a digital picture is taken, tiny silicon pixels on the memory card are activated by light, thus producing an electrical charge that forms the digital image. Since ghosts and spirits are electromagnetic energy, they are able to affect electrical devices such as cameras and memory cards. The electrical charges they emit can also impress images on the memory card as well as within the vibrational frequency of the camera's eye. As a result, digital cameras capture anomalies such as orbs, ecto-mist, vortexes, and ghosts more often because the images are electromagnetic as opposed to the film camera that relies on silver halide crystals for imprinting an image on film.

Digital images can be viewed anywhere you are and at any time you desire. This gives you the ability to save and protect your valuable results. Digital cameras also offer the option to delete unwanted images, thereby freeing up your memory card for more pictures. I would like to offer a word of caution, however. I used to delete photos before loading them onto the computer. Never again! After putting them on the computer, I was amazed at how many anomalies go unnoticed by viewing the camera screen alone. Enlargements also reveal things that were not seen on the screen. So instead of bemoaning what I might have lost, I simply purchased another memory card to eliminate the need to delete pictures until after I was sure they did not have any valuable paranormal images on them. The extra memory card has proven to be a very wise investment for me.

Tip: When I take pictures, I do so without regard to the traditional way of photographing people, places, and things. I simply point and shoot! Sometimes I take as many as two hundred or more pictures before ever looking at the screen. I take pictures in all directions (up as well as down), in front of me, behind me, and beside me. I may take as many as four hundred-plus pictures while on an investigation or field trip. Ghosts are naturally curious and they are always near us. The challenge is to catch them unawares. I may only have a few with positive results, but those are usually well worth my time and effort, and some are absolutely beyond comparison.

Sony has a camera with an infrared night-shot feature that enables you to photograph in the dark and see beyond what the human eye can see. This is an amazing camera that produces amazing results. I highly recommend the "Sony Cyber-shot" camera for nighttime photographing of paranormal phenomena, as well as the "Kodak Easy Share" digital camera as an all-around affordable ghost-hunting tool. I use it almost daily and have never been disappointed with the results.

Have fun with your digital cameras and take along plenty of rechargeable batteries because if you are having fun, chances are the ghost will be having fun also and all too often at the expense of your technical equipment. They can drain the power from your batteries, which is a sure sign they are there!

Video Camcorders

Any video camcorder, analog or digital, will work well for capturing anomalies on video. However, I feel the best camcorders are those that have night settings for filming in the dark and low-light situations. Again, Sony has developed night–vision technology that has infrared night vision features. This is an excellent feature because it will record video in very low light for several feet into the darkness. I have had great success with Sony's night-shot capabilities.

Video cameras are a valuable asset when used in the documentation of witness accounts, full coverage of the site being investigated, and recording paranormal activity. Strategically placed, they will capture events as they occur. They can be carried with you, placed on a tripod, and left to record in an area that is known to be active. I can tell you from firsthand experience that it is exciting to see orbs moving at incredible speeds, unique energy patterns as they form, and unexplained shadows dart across the screen.

I consider video camcorders to be excellent tools for any investigation. Unlike a still camera, they provide us with constant visual and audio surveillance. Being able to review and observe paranormal activity as it manifests provides unquestionable proof of ghosts. Videos show the time the activity began as well as how long it lasted. It will also document what is happening, the conditions of the surrounding area, the phenomenom itself, and possibly even the cause of the activity. Of course, having a full apparition walk in front of your camera would be the ultimate reward for ghost hunter and researcher alike.

Thermometer

Ghosts have always been associated with sudden temperature changes. Cold spots are frequently found in structures where there is paranormal activity. These abnormal cold spots are created as ghosts deplete the surrounding area of electromagnetic energy. They draw the energy from electrical outlets, appliances, and even our own auras as they attempt to manifest or create paranormal disturbances such as moving objects, opening and closing doors, making noise, and creating currents of cold air. Many cold spots are short-lived and they tend to move around rather rapidly. When an area seems to be dramatically cooler than the surrounding area, you will probably want to document this information. This can be done in a couple of ways. First, written documentation is always advisable. Second, you may want to use a device that has been designed to detect a temperature variance.

Cold spots are a sure sign of ghostly manifestations and these activities are measurable with the right equipment. When searching for ghosts, other than walking into one, you will need something to help determine where they are.

I lived in a house that had a resident ghost, and I was forever walking into cold spots. When I say cold spots, these were unnaturally cold. It felt as if I was stepping into a pool of ice water up to my knees. This was very disconcerting and always made chills run up and down my spine. I just could never get accustomed to running into ghosts at every turn. This was in the late 1980s and I had no way to measure the temperature of a suspected area of activity at that time. We eventually moved because our daughter was so frightened by the sudden unexpected drops in temperature.

I now use a noncontact laser thermometer to measure cold spots and hot spots. It has infrared capabilities and instantly tells me the temperature of whatever it is pointed at. Thermometers send out infrared beams that bounce back when making contact with a surface. This instrument will display the temperature of the reflected surface, making it easy to scan an entire room. It will certainly be an asset to your investigations, so include one in your tool chest.

Before the beginning of an investigation, it is always wise to record the temperature of the site or area you are going to investigate. Ghosts will cause drops in temperature that can average anywhere from ten degrees to fifty degrees Fahrenheit and in some extreme cases even more. I have seen drops from ninety-three degrees on a hot sultry night to minus thirteen degrees. Wow, what an exciting event, especially when we were able to photograph a huge luminous orb at least five feet wide. As an added bonus we were able to get an EVP at the same location that was very clear and graphic as well. When cold spots are encountered, I highly recommend that you take pictures in that area and also anywhere a draft is felt.

The use of a thermometer or laser scanner on field trips and investigations will definitely enhance your chances of making contact with unseen energies.

Compass

A compass is a very useful instrument to carry with you on an investigation due to its compact size and low cost. It makes for an inexpensive alternative to the more costly EMF detector. A compass will indicate a ghostly presence when the needle begins to spin erratically. Paranormal activity created by ghosts will cause the needle to turn away from the magnetic north by twenty-five to thirty degrees.

The only downside of using a compass during a ghost hunt or investigation is that it has no light and you must know the direction of the magnetic north. It requires interaction with you; however, its availability and value should not be overlooked when assembling a tool kit.

Motion Detectors

Motion detectors are yet another investigative tool used by paranormal researchers and ghost hunters alike. These monitors can alert you to movement in an area where there should be no activity. They offer an excellent way to tell if something or someone is moving about in another room while you are investigating another part of the structure. As we investigate room to room, we leave a detector behind to alert us to new activity in the cleared area. This is a great tool for indoor investigations, as an entire room or hallway can be monitored easily with this device.

Motion detectors are very sensitive and sense movement of invisible energies, ghosts, and spirits as well. They project an infrared beam; when the beam encounters movement of any kind, an alarm will sound that can be heard from another room. This alarm is an indication that there is a ghostly presence in the room. Most detectors come with an option for setting the sensor to sound an alarm or chime as it is activated. Many ghost hunters and researchers prefer the chime mode as it is softer and does not startle everyone when it's triggered.

Most sensors are battery operated and not at all expensive to purchase. Since they are so affordable, you can keep several on hand for larger investigations.

Ghost Catchers

Many ghost hunters use a very inexpensive form of motion detection. The use of small, delicate, lightweight aluminum chimes can alert you to spirited areas of activity. They can be placed anywhere to detect energy as it passes by. They can be hung in doorways, hallways, in the middle of rooms, and near suspected areas of paranormal activity. As always, the use of your own intuition will direct you to the best place to position them.

Chimes are one of my personal favorites because of their easy use and also because ghosts like to play with them. Ghosts are as curious as you and Ime and it doesn't take much energy to create a disturbance with chimes. Try these on your next investigation and you may be surprised at the result.

Electromagnetic Field Detectors

Usually referred to as EMF meters, these energy detectors will add another dimension to ghost hunting and paranormal investigations. They are easy to use and an important piece of equipment that should be included in every ghost-hunter's tool kit. They are essential for detecting invisible energies generated by ghosts. EMF meters detect the presence of electromagnetic fields and frequencies that are outside the normal range of our fine innate senses. They can successfully lead you to an area of paranormal activity as well as introduce you to other dimensions of energy and vibrational frequencies.

Natural as well as artificial fields will affect an energy reading. It's advisable to look for natural sources first whenever something is detected with your meter. Television sets, appliances, electrical wires, and water pipes can all disrupt your energy reading, especially when hidden in walls or when the building has an unusual structural design.

EMF meters detect fluctuations in the electromagnetic fields of a space as well as in weak moving fields that appear to have no discernible source. Spirits and ghosts can disrupt surrounding fields of energy during any investigation, while on a field trip, or at a paranormal research site. They have no boundaries and are often very eager to communicate. You can easily discern their presence with your meter as you will begin to receive a higher-than-average reading.

When beginning an investigation, you can easily scan an area or a room by walking around with your meter in hand. Walk slowly back and forth sweeping the area. As you walk, move your meter from top to bottom to detect moving energy forms. A ghostly presence will seldom remain still for very long periods of time.

EMF meters can also be placed in stationary positions that yield excellent results. Strategically placed on stairways, in corners, chairs, and on flat surfaces, they can detect ghosts as they pass by. An audible alarm is a useful feature and will alert you to a ghostly presence without having to keep your eyes on the meter at all times. This is a helpful way of using your meter, especially on unusually long or overnight investigations. It gives you an opportunity to rest as opposed to constantly walking around.

Ghosts seem to dissipate rapidly, and even when your meter spikes there is no guarantee that they will remain in that specific place. They may only be passing by or watching to see what you are doing. They often fade within seconds, especially if they have not absorbed enough energy to maintain their form.

Ghosts are not easily tracked and are just as hard to photograph; however, this has been accomplished. Patience and endurance often deliver their own rewards in the form of an EVP or an exciting photograph that gives evidence of life after death.

Several EMF meters are used in ghost hunting and paranormal research. They are all very effective in detecting energy fields as well as magnetic fields. The favorite for most ghost hunters are the multiple field meters that measure two or three different fields at once. They usually feature fast-reacting needle gauges and are very sensitive. The combined magnetic and electric field meters are known as Gauss meters. The milligauss (mG) is the common unit of measurement for magnetic fields and is used to measure how hard the encountered field is pushing electrons.

Still other EMF meters have a digital display; although more expensive, the digital display will give you an exact reading. They also have a light feature so you can see the reading in the dark. Meters offer various ways of displaying energy readings. Some have colored light displays allowing you to discern the range in which a disturbance occurs, usually 2 to 7 milligauss. Others have a sensitive needle that moves back and forth and also gives excellent readings. On most tracking devices, a reading of 2 is the weakest and a reading of 7 is the strongest on the meter. What distinguishes one meter from another is the sensitivity to the electromagnetic field of energy.

Before investing in an EMF meter, I suggest trying out a few to see which one seems the most comfortable for you to use. As they require you to hold them, this limits your ability to do other things such as take photographs or hold flashlights and other equipment. Only buy what you feel comfortable using. Many models now come with neck straps so the meter will be readily available when you want to use it. Either way they are an asset to any investigation and I highly recommend their use.

Dowsing Rods

The word *dowsing* means to use a tool such as a pendulum or dowsing rods to locate something. Used for centuries by many different cultures, dowsing rods have proven to be a simple, effective method of locating underground water sources, minerals, lost objects, and even money. Today dowsers are being used by water well companies, oil drillers, mining operations, and even law enforcement agencies. Skilled dowsers are in demand now more than ever.

In the past few years, dowsing has gained a new audience. The "New Age" movement introduced dowsing as a method of testing the compatibility of everything from medicine to herbs to determine what was best for our bodies. Dowsing is also used in medical diagnosis and healing as well as chakra balancing. More recently we see dowsing enter the scope of ghost hunting and paranormal research. Investigators are successful in finding unmarked graves, locating areas of strong paranormal activity, communications with spirit, and of course contact with ghosts.

Dowsing rods are very accurate tools for ghost hunting. They act as an antenna that picks up fluctuating degrees of vibrational frequencies that are also picked up by us intuitively. Simply put, dowsing is an innate ability to sense a target using dowsing rods as an extension of ourselves. They enhance our ability to react to information acquired through our personal energy system. As information enters our subconscious, we respond by involuntarily directing the rods in the direction of the target. You may feel a tingling sensation, trembling, or heat as you approach the target. These responses signify that you are going in the right direction or you are getting correct information.

Everyone is born with the innate ability to dowse. Some will respond to dowsing immediately, while others may have to practice for a while before they see results. When you dowse for a target, you tune in to its frequency. When dowsing for ghosts or to receive answers from the spirit realm, you will be entering their energy field and the rods will reflect back their frequency transmission for you to interpret.

Tree branches were probably the oldest tool used for dowsing and were used in many other countries as well as our own. Also known as "wishing sticks" or "divining rods," dowsing tools were Y-shaped branches taken from willow, hazel, or ash trees. The tree's energy enhanced the dowser's ability to work.

When using a Y-shaped tree branch, grasp the short ends of the branch with each hand. By bending your hands outward, the branch turns into a very subtle system with its extension moving up and down to indicate its target or as a response to a yes or no question.

Concentration is essential to dowsing, and you must clear your mind of any negative thoughts. Hold the rods in a way that is comfortable to you, so they can turn completely around in a circle without touching your body. While holding the rods, walk around the area to be investigated and follow the direction the rods point you to.

Crossing rods indicate confirmation. Dowsing rods may spin or turn right or left in parallel unison. They may spin clockwise or counterclockwise in response to a question. With dowsing rods, practice really does make perfect.

Begin by checking new rods for a yes or no answer. Ghosts respond readily to direct questions with simple yes or no answers. As you hold your rods, ask which way means yes; they may cross or they may spread apart. This will be your answer and of course the other direction will be a no answer. After you have determined your rods' yes and no responses, you will be ready to use them on an investigation, ghost hunt, or in cemetery research.

Collaborating evidence can be gathered with the use of dowsing rods. If the rods spin around and then suddenly stop and point in a specific direction, they may be trying to tell you something important. It could be a direction in which you should proceed, or the ghost may be trying to draw your attention to a particular room, picture, doorway, or even a grave, but most certainly it will be something you need to see.

Dowsing rods can be used on any investigation as well as in paranormal research. They can be used in buildings, new structures, restaurants, hotels, on battlefields, and in cemeteries. Inside or outside, there are no boundaries or limits as to where dowsing rods can be used.

Dowsing rods are particularly valuable to genealogists and ghost hunters when trying to locate lost or hidden graves. When dowsing an undetermined gravesite, you can ask questions to determine dates, names, how the person died, and when they were buried there. Remember to ask direct yes or no questions such as "Are you male or female?" If you intuitively feel that it is a child, ask if they are a boy or girl and if they are young or old. When trying to discern the age of a ghost, it is helpful to ask in increments of five years at a time—five years of age, ten years of age, and so on—until you arrive at an affirmative answer.

As you become more experienced with the question-and-answer process, you will be able to formulate your own questions to meet the needs of the investigation. This is especially important when in direct communication with a ghost. Questions such as "Were you murdered?" "Did you die tragically?" "Did you commit suicide?" or "Did you die naturally?" can be answered effectively with the use of dowsing rods. Again, remember to work slowly, speak naturally, and as always, be prepared to expect the unexpected. The ghost you are communicating with may have a secret to share with you or something intriguing to tell you. Remain open to any and all responses as it will add validity to the proof you are seeking.

Relax as you ask questions, work slowly and deliberately, and enjoy your experience with your dowsing rods. The ghosts will be watching you and will try to communicate with you. Be patient and allow them the opportunity to make themselves known. You will not be disappointed!

Electronic Voice Phenomena (EVP)

This phenomenon is recognized as spirit voices and the sounds and noises are often associated with a ghostly presence. Although EVPs are unusual and extraordinary, they are no longer uncommon or as rare as one might think. Discarnate spirits and departed loved ones have been leaving recorded messages for decades. Many people have answered their telephones to find the voice of their deceased loved one on the other end of the line. People are receiving messages through their cell phones without a callback number showing up. As technology taps into higher and more subtle frequencies, I believe that contact and communication with spirits will increase rapidly.

Voices have been recorded unawares on tape recorders, during news broadcasts, and through ham radios, video equipment, and even walkie-talkies. These mysterious, subtle voice transmissions sometimes seem to be heard when least expected, and sometimes it is the last person you would expect to hear from. They clearly want to be heard and to leave messages telling the world, "Hey, we have not gone anywhere! We are still here. We are only a vibration away."

Unexpected Recordings

A most unusual EVP was recorded recently during a séance; my daughter decided to take photographs during the séance with a group of friends. Only expecting to photograph orbs or perhaps ecto-mist, she was surprised, as we all were, to learn that she had inadvertently captured a male voice on her digital camera. Her Kodak digital camera has a video/audio mode, and as she was turning it off and on in the dark, she didn't realize that at some point during the event she had turned the switch to the video setting. During the course of the séance, the medium asked one of the participants to stand up. On the video clip we clearly hear the medium asking her to stand, and then a male voice said, "I *am* standing here!" He goes on to say, "I saw you take it," to which he added, "I hate you." We were stunned, to say the least. We were totally unaware of this voice transmission until we put the pictures on our computer the next day. No doubt much more would have been heard had she not switched her camera off. This just goes to show that you should always expect the unexpected, and this goes for all aspects of ghost hunting and paranormal research. Although the séance was just spiritualist friends getting together, it yielded an extraordinary communication from another realm of existence.

NOTE: We use the Kodak CX7430 digital camera with great results for photographs having captured orbs, ectomist, even a full apparition and now obviously EVPs. In my estimation it is an excellent camera for beginners and seasoned ghost hunters as well.

Digital Voice Recorders

Thomas Edison, a man of great prolific knowledge, believed futuristic technology would one day enable us to communicate directly with the dead. He even went so far as to propose that spirits would initiate communication through electronic means. He invented a device he called a "spirit phone" in hopes of establishing a way to communicate with ghosts. With today's technology, it's not hard to envision his prediction as a reality.

The introduction of digital technology has greatly improved the quality of recordings. We use at least three digital recorders on every investigation; they are connected to small tripods for stability. The recorders are connected to external microphones that provide better sound reception.

Digital voice recorders are great tools to use on every investigation or ghost hunt. They are small, easy to carry, and may have voice-activated features. They are especially good for interviews and note taking, and I really enjoy this as it eliminates something else to keep up with, namely paper, pads, and pens. It's not unusual or unheard of to find that a ghost has left you a message while you were going about the routine of interviewing a homeowner or recording your investigative data.

Digital recorders provide an excellent way to make contact with ghosts and set up an atmosphere conducive to paranormal communication. They can document proof that energy and consciousness continue to exist in all their varied forms. Ghosts can hear us. We can hear them. They want us to hear them. So set up your recorders and, as always, expect the unexpected.

Two-Way Radios
Two-way radios are absolutely necessary for staying in close communication during an investigation. When you are called to investigate extremely large areas such as train stations, hospitals, historical hotels, prisons, or castles,

it is very wise to have devices on hand that will give you peace of mind. Knowing that you can contact other team members if you find yourself in frightening or dangerous situations can be very comforting, especially if you will be working in total darkness most of the time. You will probably split up into groups of two or three, so be sure to have enough radios to go around.

Almost any two-way radio will be effective for supportive communication. We use radios that allow us to send and receive messages over distances of up to two miles. The channels are all set at the same frequency by the team leader to eliminate any confusion and guarantee effectiveness. You can also use earpieces to allow for ease of handling and hands-free communication. Two-way radios are a wise investment and should be included in any ghost hunter's tool kit.

NOTE: You may be able to pick up or tune in to a ghostly frequency with your radios. On one particular investigation, we could hear a child laughing and what seemed to be crying in the background. This occurred at the beginning of our investigation as we were getting organized and it certainly was not expected or anticipated. Interference such as this is not as uncommon as you might think.

Have fun building your tool kit. Experiment with various kinds of ghost-hunting equipment. See what works best for you. Choose what you feel the most comfortable using, especially in the dark. The best tools, of course, are the ones that will complement your own innate intuition, so trust your intuition when choosing your tools.

SEVENTEEN

A GHOSTLY INVITATION

Yet call not this long life, but think that I am,
by being dead, immortal;
Can ghosts die?

JOHN DONNE (1572–1631)

As I was considering the conclusion of this book, both of my guides came through in unison. They spiritually directed me to add this chapter, which they assure me will be beneficial to the reader. So, trusting their messages as I always do, here we go, down the rabbit hole!

Our family members, loved ones, and even our ancestors leave behind precious relics as reminders of their lives on earth. These possessions come in every shape, form, and color imaginable. They exist for one reason and one reason only—to evoke memories.

Have you ever wondered why things are left behind after your loved ones are gone? Why some things are taken by family members and other things simply disappear? Have you ever thought, perhaps in anger, that this person or that person did not deserve what they took or inherited or were given? If you have, you are not alone. However, there are no mistakes in our universe and the same laws govern us all, including ghosts.

If you have a token of remembrance that was left by a loved one, rest assured you are supposed to have it. If someone else was the recipient of something you felt you were entitled to, remember that there was probably a lesson attached to that item and it was not meant for you. Everyone who passes through the veil of vibrational frequencies during death has the ability, if their intent and desire is strong enough, to visit their own funerals, stay and console their loved ones, and even influence where and to whom their belongings are to go. The soul, after crossing over, remembers its possessions, especially favored items and cherished belongings, and is able to maintain an energy connection to them. Perhaps you have a music box that plays on its own, a picture that keeps moving around, a treasured piece of jewelry that keeps disappearing and reappearing. If so, you are in contact with its previous owner.

As a ghost or discarnate soul, they are not trying to scare us but are trying to get our attention. They want to share the message that they are not dead, are not gone. They are merely transformed into a higher vibration that is too fine for us to see. They are not stuck in heaven nor are they stuffed down in hell. They are with us every hour of every day for our entire lives. To me this is very comforting. Remember, heaven and hell are states of consciousness, not the physical states that religion would dictate we believe. This belief limits our ability to accept ghosts and paranormal activity for what they are: souls in glorified, energized bodies seeking to communicate with those they have left behind.

Perhaps ghosts are confused at times and may not understand the frequency in which they find themselves. This may be perceived as a haunting due to the fact that the ghost who is seeking recognition does not understand how to effectively communicate its needs. Time, love, and compassionate understanding will eventually draw them closer to their spiritual awakening.

If we truly desire to capture a ghost in a photograph, record their voices as an EVP, or experience them in one of their various energy forms, we will need to take the necessary steps to welcome them back into our realm of existence. To begin, choose a favorite antique, piece of jewelry, precious photograph, or something that will directly link you to the person with whom you wish to make contact. Set aside a special place to display your item. Choose a place that is away from family traffic, a place where it can remain in the background of physical activity.

If your desire is to capture your loved one's spirit on film, ask them to join you as you begin taking pictures. I recommend taking several pictures in rapid succession (digital cameras are great for this), as you will be able to see spirit take form from one shot to the next. One picture may have nothing, the next something, and the next nothing.

This is proof positive that you have indeed had a visitation. Spirit can and does respond to telepathic messages. You may feel a little silly talking to a ring or a picture, but I assure you they will hear you and in time they will respond. You may be able to photograph ectoplasm, orbs, a vortex, or, if you're lucky, a fully energized form. I used the word "lucky" because it takes a lot of energy to manifest due to the density of our atmosphere. However, this is possible and happens more frequently than people are aware. You may also hear a voice and be able to respond telepathically. Please, at this point don't begin to question what you see and hear, as this is the greatest detriment to spiritual contact. Make an effort to accept it as part of your ever-changing spiritual reality. By acknowledging your contact, you will pave the way for future visitations. You may also feel goose bumps, which is always significant and should never be discounted, because they are definitely associated with a ghostly presence.

In the 1950s, EVPs entered the field of paranormal research. Serious studies and investigations began to try to understand spirit communication. However, it was a controversial undertaking and remains so to this day. Since science demands proof by repeated performance, this creates a problem. Due to the fields of energy and vibrational frequencies that must be accessed, EVPs may always remain a questionable event. We do not yet have the required knowledge and technology to expand this field of research and also to satisfy strict scientific criteria at the same time.

If you have experienced an EVP recording, however, you will be forever changed, and suddenly science and its demand for proof will not be able to affect the truth that has been revealed to you. If you have heard a loved one's voice from beyond; received an answer to a question asked during an investigation; or just spontaneously and unexpectedly heard a voice come through your car radio, television set, computer, or over your phone, you can never go back to believing as you did before. Your belief system will have to be adjusted, and when this happens new insights will lead you through mysterious doorways of thought into higher spiritual dimensions. You will relate to energy and vibrations on a new level, and this understanding will lead you to accept the fact that *there is no death and we do not die.*

Skeptics would have us believe that an EVP is probably radio frequency interference or something as strange as extraterrestrial attempts at communication. Imagine that! They would rather believe in aliens than ghosts. Some skeptics believe that we project our own imagination into discerning what is heard and then we tell someone else, thus creating a message that everyone understands as the same thing.

Why is it so hard to believe the truth? Because when you believe, you have to face the truth of your reality. Are you prepared to do that? Not many people are. I salute ghost hunters and investigators everywhere, because on some level they are aware that as energy we will always exist. Keep up the good work!

EVPs are best explained as inter-dimensional communication. They may be heard as whispers, singing, crying, or muffled angry voices. They can be recorded everywhere and anywhere, inside and outside of structures. We recorded an EVP in an abandoned train station that was not at all what we expected to hear and certainly out of character for its surroundings, or so it seemed at the time.

After a long investigation at the train station, we returned home to put our photos and digital recordings on the computer. After a period of hearing no sounds at all, we could hardly stay awake and had almost decided to call it a night. Then we heard it! We were astonished to hear a male voice say, "Get her now!" Of course we were eerily affected by the sound of his voice and naturally assumed he was talking about one of us. However, further communication revealed a more sinister transmission. The second thing we heard was a female voice screaming, "Help me!" This was followed by a high-pitched, fearful scream of "Help me! Rape!" And then she screamed "Rape!" again. After a short time of hearing nothing, we heard a blood-curdling scream and then a deadly silence. We sat there in the quiet of the early morning hours shocked and perplexed at what we had heard.

What exactly had we heard? Obviously we had an excellent EVP that was so clear and distinct that no one would even have to analyze it for clarity. Even more obvious was the fact that the traumatic event was forever impressed in the etheric realm of the train station. What we had recorded was a *residual haunting*. This type of event is usually left as an energy imprint paralyzed by time. It replays itself over and over again until eventually its energy dissipates. This could take years or even centuries to occur, depending on its emotional or traumatic influence. This recording was totally unexpected, and we are in the process of trying to research a possible rape/murder that could have happened at the train station. Of course it could have happened years before the train station was built. A residual haunting can be attached to the property and not necessarily to the structure itself. Most of our EVPs were recorded in the old segregated area of the train station. We were also able to record gospel singing, children playing and crying, as well as the sounds and noises associated with a busy train station.

We never try to second-guess a recording. We can either hear and understand it clearly or not at all. We may hear strange noises, bizarre voices, childhood chatter, and even different languages. If it's clear and concise, no one will have to guess, imagine, or wonder if the communication is real. Team members and skeptics alike will recognize it easily as a voice from another realm of existence.

You may wish to attempt recording an EVP at night. Sound travels through frequencies at different levels during the day and at night. I have had better luck (there is that word again) between the hours of midnight and four AM. As before, place your recorder near or next to a cherished photograph, a treasured antique, or some token remembrance of a loved one that holds deep sentimental value for you. They will be watching your activities as you set up your equipment and will know that you want to hear from them. They see and hear us easily and are anxious to respond to our requests. We've only to ask.

It's important to remember that ghosts are people who are invisible to us; it is their voices we hear. It's easy to converse with them either telepathically or verbally just as if they were standing next to us, which, by the way, they sometimes are. Although I leave my recorder in one place, other members of our team are comfortable walking around and asking questions while carrying their recorders with them. During an investigation, these question-and-answer sessions are often very successful for them. They have engaged in dialogue on occasion and this is very exciting.

If you have decided to carry a recorder, it is always helpful to follow some guidelines for the best results. Never whisper; speak just as you normally do. Spirit voices are sometimes faster or slower than normal speech, so their voices can be easily distinguished from others.

It is also helpful to ask questions in a yes-or-no format. Always pause between questions to give the spirit ample time to answer. You might want to phrase your questions like these examples: "What is your name?" "When did you die?" "How old are you?" "Where did you die?" Try to formulate your questions so ghosts or spirits can answer using the least number of words possible. This is especially helpful in cemeteries where there are not enough power sources for ghosts to draw their energy. It takes a lot of energy to communicate, and they may not be able to sustain energy long enough to communicate their message.

To capture a spirit on film or record their voice after making a request is extremely empowering and spiritually uplifting. You will never be the same again; you will find that spiritual doors will open in abundance, enticing you to higher understandings of your own spirituality. You will no doubt lose all fear of death and find that peace, love, and joy have replaced any confusion in your life.

Keep your cameras and recorders handy, and get ready to embark on the journey of a lifetime.

EIGHTEEN

GHOSTLY CONVERSATIONS

Then away out in the woods I heard that kind of a sound that a ghost makes when it wants to tell about something that is on its mind and can't make itself understood, and so can't rest easy in its grave, and has to go about that way every night grieving.

MARK TWAIN (1835–1910)

Can we communicate with ghosts? Can they understand us as well as see us? Can we understand them?

At some point in your ghost-hunting quest, you may have the opportunity to communicate with a ghost. If the time and place are conducive, it is very possible to have a clear exchange of thoughts. If you are patient and sincere in your desire and intent, you may hear from a ghost or at least be able to capture their voice on a recorder. Their thoughts will manifest as sounds, and these sounds may eventually become discernible words.

If the ghost feels comfortable with you and your equipment, this could set up a situation conducive for full materialization. Be very sure you can handle this interaction. Do *not* do this for fun and games. Be respectful and try to appreciate the fact that this is not an easy task for ghosts.

Usually when this type of contact is made, it will be from either a ghost or a spirit who has transitioned to a much higher plane of existence. You will be communicating with an intelligent energy form that is fully capable of interacting on a conscious level. They are aware of death, and they are aware that they are no longer connected to any dimension. They will be free spirits.

It is very easy for us to communicate with those in higher dimensions because of our telepathic abilities, which allow thought to travel through vibrational frequencies at tremendous speeds. Usually, if you are able to receive spirit communication, it will be from your right ear. Your right eardrum will vibrate as super-high frequencies make contact. As a prelude to a ghostly voice, you may hear ringing in your right ear.

Different sounds and tones will bring your brain waves into a state of greater receptivity. The ghost may create these frequencies and unusual sounds to help you. If you hear weird high-pitched noises, humming, or buzzing, there is a good chance that you are accepting these vibrations, and ghostly voices may follow. As the vibrational rate of the electromagnetic field rises, the brain generates tremendous electrical charges that are greater than normal, allowing you to hear sounds and voices that would otherwise be mute to you.

You may be communicating and not even realize it. Pay attention to your thoughts. Are they really your thoughts? Listen to your inner voice. Is it yours or theirs? Do you hear a male voice or a female voice? Is it an adult voice or that of a child? Note the difference between any male and female voices you hear. Female voices may sound sadder and more emotional, even distraught. Male voices will be stronger and louder, and perhaps even angry.

You may hear or record more female voices in old houses as they are usually the ghostly caretakers of these energized structures. They are also more likely to be heard in libraries, nurseries, hospitals, and schools. They are often shy and may try to communicate just as you are preparing to leave. Their messages may also be symbolic in nature. Female ghosts have a unique way of communicating that will distinguish them from their male counterparts. You may encounter male voices in cemeteries, inside old buildings and castles, at historical sites, and on battlefields. They may contact you immediately and let you know that you are not alone. They may try to frighten you away by shouting "Leave!" or "Go!"

With all of this in mind, the following is a set of guidelines for you to follow when attempting to communicate with a spirit or ghost.

Telepathy is an awareness of information and emotions that exist in the mind of another (even a ghost). This is a very real form of communication and one that you may experience from time to time. The objective is to learn what motivates the ghost to be in the house, building, cemetery, or wherever you may encounter it.

If the prospect of talking to a ghost makes you nervous, you may want to practice first. Just pretend that you are interviewing a real person. You must first decide where you would like to hold your interview. Preferably this would be a place where a ghostly encounter has occurred. You are aware that they are there and they are also aware of your presence. You can schedule an appointment by stating your intention for a personal interview, literally face to face albeit with an invisible guest.

Do your research beforehand. If you plan the interview in a house, find out as much as possible about the house. Research the history of the house, the families who have lived there, and historical events that may have taken place there. The same process holds true for all buildings, churches, and hospitals.

If you plan an interview in a cemetery, you will want to know as much as possible about the cemetery. How many men, women, and children are buried there? Local genealogy societies have a wealth of information to share and searching their records will benefit you greatly. Having background knowledge will give you greater self-confidence and will help you formulate your questions.

Prepare to spend at least thirty minutes on the actual interview. This will give you plenty of time to ask questions and wait patiently for the answers. You will be interviewing them in their own environment so this should allow them the freedom to communicate with you, if they have a desire to do so.

Remember to dress as comfortably as possible. You will probably be a little anxious with your first interview and will want to be as relaxed as possible. Wear comfortable supportive shoes, especially if you will be walking in the dark. Of course, bring along a flashlight and plenty of batteries. If you successfully make contact with someone who wishes to communicate with you, they will need energy to maintain their conversation and may drain your batteries in the process.

Do *not* ask silly questions! This will show the ghost that you are not serious and may result in a "dead" interview. It is always best to prepare your questions ahead of time based on your research and knowledge of who you are seeking to communicate with. Listen carefully and establish a relaxed style of questioning. Make your questions brief and to the point. As you allow your questions to flow, you will want to interject long pauses, which will give the ghosts time to manifest an answer.

New questions may arise as communication is established. They may mention something that you are unaware of, or they may want to tell you some long-forgotten secret. Despite all your research, there is usually something left to uncover.

Remember, they will know ahead of time that you are coming and what your intentions are; they may be a lot more prepared for the actual interview than you are.

It is always a good idea to have a team member with you. This gives you added security, and you will also have a witness to any paranormal events as they unfold. You will want to carry a notebook and pen and either a cassette recorder or a digital recorder. Of course plenty of batteries are a must. Always use new tapes and never tape over other voices. This may be your one and only chance to record a ghost from another dimension and you would not want to lose it.

Holding your recorder in your non-writing hand allows you to operate the on and off buttons and to write notes with the other hand. Having a notebook also allows you to document your thoughts and feelings, as they play a crucial part in the interview whether you are aware of it or not. You will want to record any sights, sounds, or smells you may experience. Also, anything out of the ordinary that happens is extremely important. For instance, if a dove were to land near you, there could be a ghost named "Dove" who wishes to communicate with you. Trust your intuition and do not ignore or pass off anything as a coincidence.

If you do get an audible or telepathic response to your questions, listen carefully to what is being said. Try to discern the answer. If you don't understand something, don't be afraid to ask. Perhaps you could ask them to respond in a simpler way or clarify what was said. You may take on the role of a detective as you try to figure out brief replies, angry responses, or faint whispers. Patience is the key to discerning their messages.

If at all possible, ask open-ended questions that can be answered with a simple yes or no. It is always helpful to begin your questions with who, what, when, where, or how. "When did you die?" "How old are you?" "What is your name?" Questions such as these will open the door to future communication. If a ghost is evasive or doesn't seem to want to answer your questions, you may want to reword it. Perhaps they just don't understand. Of course, they could also speak a different language and simply not understand your questions.

Always have your camera on hand to take photographs. At the beginning of an interview and at the end are excellent times to ask for permission to photograph them. If the interview went well, you may be rewarded with a great photograph to take home with you, along with a successful EVP.

I have two interviews scheduled in the near future. One is with the ghost at the old antebellum house and the other is with the ghost at the abandoned train station. While other members of our team are busy setting up equipment, I will be interviewing my ghosts. Hopefully I will leave with a better understanding of who they represent, why they approached me, and what it is that they want to communicate.

Will I look silly talking to thin air? Probably! Will my team support me? Absolutely! Will I be able to establish communication? You just never know! But I know one thing for sure: I am always prepared to expect the unexpected!

NINETEEN

THE ULTIMATE GHOST TALE

Human beings, vegetable, or cosmic dust,
we all dance to a mysterious tune,
intoned in the distance by an invisible player.

ALBERT EINSTEIN (1879–1955)

Many years ago, before I accepted my gifts of clairvoyance and clairaudience, I wasn't as comfortable with ghosts as I am now. The following story surfaced from my memory with such clarity that I felt that I should share it with you in closing. Although it was scary at the time, my perception of the incident is greatly altered today.

In the very rural area of Texas where I was raised, there is a graveyard, and in that graveyard is a "vampire grave"— or so the rumors go.

I visited the graveyard so often as a child and in my teenage years that it seemed like the most natural place in the world to be. We have had many picnics there, I've done genealogy research there, and all in all, we've spent a lot of time there over the years. It is a pretty, serene place surrounded by huge oak trees. It has always been a peaceful place to go, even alone. I never gave a moment's thought to ghosts or the supposed "vampires" there.

Near the back of the small, remote graveyard is a beautiful gated gravesite. It stands out prominently amid the old, encrusted, broken tombstones. The gravesite is enclosed inside an eight-foot fence with a gate that remained locked for many years. This is where our story begins.

Evidently, in the late 1800s there was a family who moved into this remote community. They couldn't speak English, except for the father who could only speak limited English at best. As we know, people always fear what they don't understand and evidently this gave rise to the tales of vampirism. Shortly after their fated arrival, they were murdered, and the townspeople buried the entire family in one grave. Perhaps guilt prompted them to enclose the gravesite—or maybe fear directed them to do so. Either way, it has stood the test of time as a monument to their tragedy.

It gets curiouser and curiouser! Late one dreary afternoon while my daughter and I were out visiting relatives, she asked me if we could stop by the "vampire graveyard." As it was on our way home, I agreed, because I really enjoyed going there myself. Although I have always felt comfortable there, I began to feel a little apprehensive as we approached the secluded entrance. It was getting cloudy and a fine misty rain seemed to be settling in. I shrugged it off as being caused by the weather and we drove inside.

I parked the car, and things began to change with such rapid force that there was no way to comprehend the events as they unfolded. We got out of the car and began to stroll around admiring the beautiful purple, flowering ground cover around some of the tombstones. Suddenly, my daughter stopped and turned around to look at me with the oddest expression on her face.

"Mother, do you hear that?" she said.

"No, what is it?" I whispered.

"It's the most beautiful music I have ever heard in my life! Can't you hear the harps?"

"Tammy, I don't hear anything and you don't hear anything, and we are getting out of here right now!"

As soon as the words were out of my mouth, she grabbed my wrists with both of her hands. It felt as if steel bands had clamped around my wrists. I stood there, rooted to the spot, unable to move! She looked at me so sweetly and said, "Mother, come with me." Are you crazy? I thought. I couldn't move. She began to pull me closer to her and then across the cemetery toward the "vampire grave." Now, I am pretty strong, and you can well imagine my distress when I couldn't even wrangle myself free of her grasp. I was terrified beyond belief! My head was spinning! What was I going to do?

"Mother, come and see, come into the light with me." As I watched her face, I noticed a mist forming all around us, and out of my peripheral vision I could see a huge white fog forming. I started to visualize us being drawn down inside a deep hole or, worse yet, into another dimension.

By now, she had literally dragged me halfway across the graveyard and nearer to the "vampire grave" than ever before. When I finally realized how close we were to the gravesite, I snapped! I tried to wiggle my wrist free of her hold. Then I yanked forcefully once more and I was free! I really hate to say this, but honesty demands that I tell the truth about this incident. As I yanked free of her grasp, I hit her, hard, right then and there! I literally knocked her out! Oh, my God, I thought, as she crumbled to the ground.

It was getting darker and a gentle rain was coming down. I managed to pick her up and carry her all the way back to where the car was parked. I got her into the car and slammed and locked the doors. I flew out of that graveyard like a maniac on a mission!

Just as we drove onto the paved road, she sat up and looked at me quizzically. "Mother, I thought we were going to the vampire graveyard. Didn't we just pass it? Gee, my jaw hurts and my face is stinging!"

"I'll explain it to you in a minute. Just give me a minute, please," I whispered.

What happened? I wish I knew! We obviously experienced ghostly paranormal activity at its most profound intensity. When I am asked if I would react differently today, I usually reply that I would like to think that I would. However, when one of your children is involved, even though they are adults, I believe it certainly affects how you will react in a situation.

Obviously we were led there for a reason. I'd like to think that today I would be able to talk to whoever was interacting with her and through her. I believe that my education in parapsychology and knowledge of paranormal events, ghosts, and spirits, as well as alternate realities, has changed my perception so that I might better understand the truth of my reality.

One thing is for sure. When I say, "Always expect the unexpected!" I speak from the voice of experience.

Until my next book...

Melba Goodwyn

GLOSSARY

Agent: A person a haunting seems to be centered on

Anomaly (Anomalies): Something found that has no explainable source; strange unrecognizable shapes appearing in photographs taken at haunted sites and cemeteries

Apparition: A disembodied spirit that appears either fully or partially visible to the human eye; may be captured in photographs

Apport: A solid object that seemingly appears out of nowhere, believed to be teleported from another dimension

Astral body: The part of an individual that is the life force, the essence of the soul of a person

Astral projection: Leaving one's body, the ability to project oneself outside the physical body

Astrology: Study of the planets in relation to human life

Aura: The electromagnetic energy field that emanates from all living things, usually in colors that reveal emotions, health, and moods

Automatic writing: Communication from spirit in written form by using a medium's hand to do the actual writing

Avatars: a bodily manifestation of a highly evolved spiritual being; usually implying a deliberate descent into lower realms of existence for a specific purpose

Benevolent: Helpful, loving intentions, passive

Bi-location: The uncommon phenomenom of a person or object appearing in two distant places simultaneously

Cemetery: Resting place for the deceased; usually near a church

Channeling: The act of allowing spirit to deliver messages from other realms through trance, automatic writing, painting, or music

Clairaudient: Psychic ability to hear sounds or voices that are inaudible to others

Clairsentience: The ability to feel things not normally felt by most people

Clairvoyance: A French term that means "clear seeing"; refers to receiving information from objects or events without using the normal senses; ability to foresee the future

Coincidences: Occurrences, within a short space of time, of two or more meaningful events without any apparent connection between them (Actually, there are no coincidences as most people perceive them to be. Everything happens for a reason and most of the time it is to facilitate our spiritual growth.)

Cold spot: An area of the electromagnetic energy field that can be free-floating or stationary

Crisis apparition: A specific type of spirit sighting during which the apparition manifests itself to a particular person; a spirit who appears to friends or loved ones at the exact moment of death

Déjà vu: An eerie feeling that one has visited a place before or has experienced some activity at an earlier time or in a past life

Demon: Evil or inhuman spirit; a low-level negative energy that interacts with evil

Discarnate: Existing without a physical body; spirits that are free of the body's restrictions

Doppelgänger: Ghosts of living people that are exact duplicates; a projected OBE, either consciously or unconsciously

Dowsing: The art of using forked sticks or dowsing rods to find graves, water, caves, oil, etc. (also known as radiesthesia)

Ecto-Mist: The second stage of ghostly manifestation; a mist or fog; spirit manifesting as mist

Electronic Voice Phenomenon (EVP): Voices captured on digital recorders when no one is present; voices of spirits who are attempting to communicate with living persons; describes noises and voices recorded on traditional audio- or videotape that are often heard during playback

EMF detector: An instrument that measures electromagnetic energy fields (also known as a Gauss meter)

Energy: A force; the essence of all creation; vibrational frequencies of creative power

Entity: Any being or beings with life force of some type, including spirits and ghosts

Exorcism: The expulsion of demons or spirits from a person or place

Extrasensory perception (ESP): An awareness of actual happenings or information not attained through the five physical senses

Field trip: An informal attempt to see or record a ghost in a location that has no history of haunting

Gauss meter: An instrument that measures electromagnetic fields

Geomagnetic field: The magnetic field around the earth; changes in this field are said to influence spirit activity

Ghost: A deceased person or image appearing to the living; visual appearance of a person who has died

Ghost hunter: Someone who looks for and documents what they believe to be ghosts or paranormal activity related to ghosts

Ghost lights: Eerie, colored lights that sometimes appear and are often photographed in haunted houses, cemeteries, on deserted roads and train tracks, in mountains and woods, and in large open areas

Globule: A tiny sphere of electromagnetic energy; spirit often appears on film as globules (also known as orbs)

Graveyard: Resting place for the dead that may be located in secluded places and may not be near a church

Hallucination: A sensory experience that does not correspond to physical reality

Haunted: Refers to a person or place to which spirits may be attached; recurrent visitation of a ghost or spirit

Haunting: Refers to an apparition that is seen, heard, and felt; associated with unexplainable phenomena

Imprint: Energy that is encased either temporarily or permanently in a dimensional frequency; energy deposit created by extreme trauma or repetitive actions over periods of time

Intelligent haunting: Ghosts who are capable of intelligent interaction; communication with ghosts

Intuition: The ability to discern a situation or event by going beyond rational or intellectual analysis; use of the sixth sense to draw conclusions

Investigation: The act of researching a location that has had a history of past paranormal activity

Levitation: The rising of an object or person with no visible means of support

Light rod: Straight, luminous beams of light; may be any color

Location: Place where paranormal activity is occurring; site of an investigation

Malevolent: Destructive, harmful, angry, frightening behavior

Manifestation: The appearance of a ghost taking form; the manner in which ghosts and spirits present themselves to us

Materialization: The deliberate, usually temporary, visible formation of a spirit or ghost

Medium: A psychic through whom spirits can communicate; someone who can communicate with spirits on behalf of another human being; trance medium

Metaphysics: Derived from the Greek word *meta* meaning "beyond"; that which is beyond the law of physics

Mysticism: Belief in a spiritual world or other dimensions that cannot be perceived visually

Numerology: The study of numbers and their vibrational influence on a person's life

Omen: A sign of things to come; to portent of the future

Orb: A sphere of electromagnetic energy produced by spirit; actual embodiment of spirit in varying sizes; representing spirit

Out-of-body experience (OBE): Experience of leaving your body for a period of time (also known as "traveling clairvoyance" and astral projection)

Paranormal: Occurrences that take place outside the natural order of things; ghosts, UFOs, ESP; difficult to explain; beyond the normal, yet in the realm of the natural; something that is beyond the range of normal human experience

Paranormal researcher: One who researches that which is beyond simple human experiences or scientific explanations

Parapsychology: Derived from the Greek word *para* meaning "beyond"; literally means "beyond psychology"; the scientific study of paranormal phenomena; the study of a phenomenon real or supposed that appears inexplicable

Phantom: An apparition or specter existing as an energy form

Poltergeist: A German term meaning "noisy ghost" linked to a living person (also known as RSPK or recurrent spontaneous psychokinesis)

Portal: Strong energy gateway between the spirit world and our world; access point to other dimensions

Precognition: Seeing or knowing what will occur in the future

Psychic: Someone who uses various forms of clairvoyance or empathic feelings to tap into nonphysical realities; someone who is sensitive to the spiritual world

Psychokinesis: The ability to move objects using one's mind

Residual ghost: A term used to describe a spirit's energy that is trapped in a continuous time loop and reenacts certain events repeatedly

Séance: A gathering of individuals, usually presided over by a medium, for the purpose of receiving spirit communication with the dead or paranormal manifestations

Sensitive: A person with psychic and empathic abilities

Shadow ghost: A black form with no discernible features that often appears in photographs as if caught unawares

Sixth sense (ESP): The acquisition of information by means beyond the five human senses

Skeptic: Someone who refuses to believe in the existence of ghosts, energy anomalies, and paranormal phenomena; one who doubts, questions, or disagrees with the existence of other dimensions

Soul: The very essence of who we are; spiritual energy encased in a physical body

Spirit: Electromagnetic energy in the form of orbs, ectomist, shadows, and full apparitions; higher vibrational energy not bound by physical restrictions

Spirit guide: A spirit who desires to help and guide its soul connections in the physical realm

Spiritualism: A movement that later became a religion centered on proving life everlasting for the spirit

Supernatural: Acts of a divine nature; something that occurs or exists through means other than the known forces of nature

Synchronicity: The interconnectedness of coincidences and their hidden meanings

Telepathy: Commonly known as an awareness of information or emotions that exist in the mind of another person; soul-to-soul communication; communication using the mind as opposed to the senses

Thought forms: Apparitions or anomalies produced by the power of thought

Vortex: A funnel of energy used by ghosts as a conveyance in which to move about easily while at the same time maintaining their energy fields

White noise: Buzzing sound formed by a combination of audible frequencies, often used as background noise for EVP recordings